SEVEN SIGNS of ST. JOHN

A REFLECTIVE JOURNAL TO DISCOVER POWER WITHIN

Jn. 12:32

*". . . When I am lifted up from the earth,
I will draw everyone to myself."*

MARGARET SHERIDAN B.Ed.

Copyright © 2010 by Margaret Sheridan B.Ed.

ISBN:		Softcover		978-1-4500-7172-7

All rights reserved. No part of this book may be reproduced or transmitted in any form or by any means, electronic or mechanical, including photocopying, recording, or by any information storage and retrieval system, without permission in writing from the copyright owner.

Scripture quotations are taken from the Holy Bible; the New American School and Church Edition. Copyright 1970, 1981, 1987, Fireside Bible Publishers, Wichita, Kansas.

This book was printed in the United States of America.

To order additional copies of this book, contact:
Xlibris Corporation
1-800-618-969
www.xlibris.com.au
Orders@xlibris.com.au
500130

SEVEN SIGNS of ST. JOHN

CONTENTS

Preface 9
Acknowledgements 11
Journaling 13
A Process To Help Contemplation 14
A Suggested Process To Read And Contemplate Scripture. 15
St. John—The Contemplative 18
An Overview Of The Seven Signs 19
Diagram of The Map of Palestine Showing Locations
    Where Jesus Performed These Signs 20
Jewish Feasts That Connect With The Signs 21

The First Sign—A Wedding in Cana 23
The Second Sign—Cure of the Nobleman's Son 43
The Third Sign—Cure of the Paralytic at Bethesda 63
The Fourth Sign—Multiplication of the Loaves 83
The Fifth Sign—Jesus Walks on the Sea 103
The Sixth Sign—Jesus Cured a Man who was Blind from Birth 123
The Seventh Sign (i)—Jesus raises Lazarus from the dead 143
The Seventh Sign (ii)—Jesus raises Lazarus from the dead 163

List of References 183

DEDICATED TO THE MEMORY OF MY PARENTS,
EVELYN AND ALLAN PEARCE
AND ALSO TO
OUR DAUGHTER, GEMMA
AND
OUR SON, BENJAMIN
FROM WHOM I HAVE DRAWN INSPIRATION.

PREFACE

Reflection on the symbolism contained in the Seven Signs that are presented in the Gospel of St. John, form the subject matter to be reflected on in this journal. The scope of this book relies on the action of the Holy Spirit who is at the centre of the person who takes up the invitation to interact with Jesus who is present in these Sacred Signs.

There is an opportunity to analyse the text, to explore theological levels and to make a personal response to challenges identified, by users of this journal. The Seven Signs are actions of Jesus, in response to individuals whom He encountered and they progressively reveal the name of God, the holiness of God and the glory or radiant beauty of God.

Through these Signs we are empowered in the here and now, to welcome Jesus and invite Him to be present and powerful in our lives. His enduring presence in the Scripture is nourishing, abiding, enlightening and fulfilling.

ACKNOWLEDGEMENTS

I gratefully acknowledge my family, my husband John, our daughter, Gemma, and our son Benjamin, my colleagues, my many students and my friends who have encouraged me to assemble this journal. In particular I thank my husband, John, for his patience, reliability and affirmation regarding the content. I also thank him for typing, proofreading and editing drafts. Our son, Benjamin's scrutiny of consistency of the layout has proved to be of great benefit.

Of particular note I acknowledge the ideas of many authors who have influenced my thoughts, values and attitudes which have contributed to the generation of this journal.

JOURNALING

Herein I keep a written account of my realisations in response to my prayerful reading of Scripture. Sometimes my responses may cause me some feelings of guilt, shame or embarrassment, but I still record these human experiences, as well as those responses that cause me peace, joy and contentment. Holy Spirit of God, be with me and teach me to be honest and to persevere with hope in developing a faithful relationship with Jesus through this process of listening, writing and doing. God the Father identified Jesus his Son, and gave us an instruction at the Transfiguration of Jesus.

> "This is my Son, the Beloved; he enjoys my favour. *Listen* to him". Matt. 17:5

> This is my Son, the Chosen One. *Listen* to him." Luke 9:35

> Mary, the mother of Jesus, has given her direction to us.

> "Do whatever he tells you." Jn 2: 5

In my journal I record by writing and drawing

—what **I have** listened to and
—what **I intend to** do

A PROCESS TO HELP CONTEMPLATION

1. I set aside a specific amount of time that suits me, (e.g. ten or twenty minutes a day).

2. I set aside a quiet place where I will not be disturbed,

   _at home
   _in my room or study
   _in my preferred environment e.g. a garden or by a water feature.

3. I follow a method of contemplation.

4. I remember that John wrote this Gospel with the image before him of the Radiant Beauty that is the Glory of the Risen Jesus, clarifying in his mind, occurrences that he had witnessed during the lifetime of Jesus and which give breadth and depth to these Seven Signs.

5. I ask the Spirit of God for the wisdom to open my heart and my mind to welcome Jesus, who is present in the Scripture.

A SUGGESTED PROCESS TO READ AND CONTEMPLATE SCRIPTURE.

1. READ: Faculties used: intellect and memory

I imagine the place and the interaction of characters that 'The Sign', the miracle happened in.

Read—I see the characters and settings in order to clarify the literal meaning.
Read—I *outline* the sequence of events by using the narrative diagram.
Read—I *highlight* words or phrases that impact on me. I verify what I 'hear.'
Read—I *observe* the characters interaction and relationships and I evaluate the relationships of the persons who are presented.

2. REFLECT: Faculties used: intellect and memory.

Reflect—I listen to my own life experiences, where God has "taken root" in my life, i.e. my relationships and interactions with others.

Reflect-insight. This 'touch of life' penetrates down through layers of my experiences until it reaches my 'centre'. I see the characters—I see the encounter where Jesus responds to . . ., persons who are like me. I take note of words or actions that 'give him away'.

3. JOURNAL: Faculties used: intellect and memory.

The action of Jesus continues in the lives of his people in the here and now. In my journal I record how this action penetrates my life and my heart.

I imagine myself as one of the characters from the "Sign" and I allow the encounter, the relationship, the interplay and the interaction to recur in me. In this way the **power** of the action of Jesus **is available** to me. I have the opportunity to communicate with Jesus at a deep level within my "inner room", where I suffer with love, wait for and am challenged by people, or situations, that I carry in my heart. This communication is possible through "becoming" one of the persons presented in the "Sign". The act of journaling the reactions and responses that happen within me, may help me, little by little, to find power to be **who I am** and to articulate what I am really looking for.

4. **RESOLVE:** Faculties used: intellect and will to make decisions. I ask for the grace to respond enthusiastically to the revelation of God's love, his intimacy, and his will and that God's name will be sanctified and that God's reign will be achieved in me, and in all people everywhere.

5. **MANDALA:** Faculties used: intellect, memory and will.

The Mandala is a design that depicts the idea of wholeness by a circle within a symmetrical square. The various elements of the Mandala, i.e. the activities and interests that have emerged during this contemplation, I arrange by drawing, so that the most important idea or the energy evoked, is at the centre of the circle and the least important activities and thoughts that relate to that centre are at the periphery of the circle. Within the Mandala, opposites are reconciled at the centre. The circumference of the circle includes all my interrelated responses from my personal world to the sign contemplated.

6. **RECAPITULATION:** Examine for each sign using the four functions of the psyche which connect with earth, air, water and fire. This is like a compass by which we can orientate ourselves to both our inner and outer worlds.

Level 1. Literal: Sensory—my emotional response. I perceive the facts through my senses—"I feel."

Level 2. Recollective, analytic meaning.—I link the facts with my own personal memories. "I think and I visualise."

Level 3. Mythic, symbolic-inferred meaning. Here I feel about the facts, I make value judgements and give viewpoints of different characters. i.e. value/worth, rational evaluation. I connect, identify and allow the encounter to recur in myself.

Level 4. Individual meaning: Integral/Religious—intuitive response, i.e. I look beyond the facts to the possibilities relevant to my time and my imagination. Through this examine, "I am energised to apply the truth discovered to live creatively. I draw my intuition of Divine action in my own life as it corresponds to the meaning of the event contemplated."

7. NOTES.

Faculties used: intellect, memory and will.

These pages leave free space for any responses that I create or recall e.g.

> **Mind: Inner thoughts.**
> **Heart: Inner beliefs**
> **Will: Inner commands**

> **My dreams: I create a mind-tape to play the phrases the elements the colours the symbols the events the motifs.**

Something I learned-

Some thing that I have allowed to become real in my life.

Some ideas and thoughts that I can share with others.

ST. JOHN—THE CONTEMPLATIVE

St John, the teacher of all the world (Jew, Gentile, Slave or Free), is represented with the Royal Eagle which can gaze unblinkingly at the sun. It was his privilege to look upon the face of God and live. He understood and loved the Word made ***flesh*** and his Gospel appeals most directly to the heart as well as the intellect. The eagle is the symbol of the Ascension of Jesus the Lord. St John has traditionally been credited with authorship of the fourth gospel, Revelation and three Epistles of the Christian Scriptures. John wrote with the image before him of the Radiant Beauty of the Risen Jesus that clarified in his mind, occurrences that he had witnessed during the lifetime of Jesus in Palestine. This perspective gave depth and breadth to his interpretation of Signs through which Jesus reveals himself to us. John uses the written account of connected events, as a means, to represent through symbol, the meaning or the message of a spiritual reality. St. John uses the word, ***sign,*** to describe an action of Jesus to ***look for*** a symbolic meaning in the account, that is, a meaning or message beyond the literal level, of a spiritual reality. Dialogue and monologue are both used to expand the symbolic importance of the sign. Here, Jesus uses metaphors which His audience understand literally only therefore Jesus teaches them the spiritual truth and theological meaning that are contained in the signs through dialogue or monologue.

AN OVERVIEW OF THE SEVEN SIGNS

1st Sign:
John 2: 1-12
A Wedding in Cana.

2nd Sign:
John 4: 43-54
The cure of the Nobleman's son at Cana, where faith of the Nobleman was required.

3rd Sign:
John 5: 1-9
The cure of the Paralytic man at the Sheep Pool at Bethesda.

4th Sign:
John 6: 1-15
The multiplication of the loaves.

5th Sign:
John 6: 16-21
Jesus walks on the sea and reveals his name, "I AM".

6th Sign:
John 9: 1-7
Jesus cures the man who was blind from birth and also reveals Himself to him as "THE ONE WHO IS SENT".

7th Sign:
John 11: 1-20
(i) Jesus raises Lazarus from the dead.

John 11:28-44
(ii) Jesus raises Lazarus from the dead.

DIAGRAM OF THE MAP OF PALESTINE SHOWING LOCATIONS WHERE JESUS PERFORMED THESE SIGNS

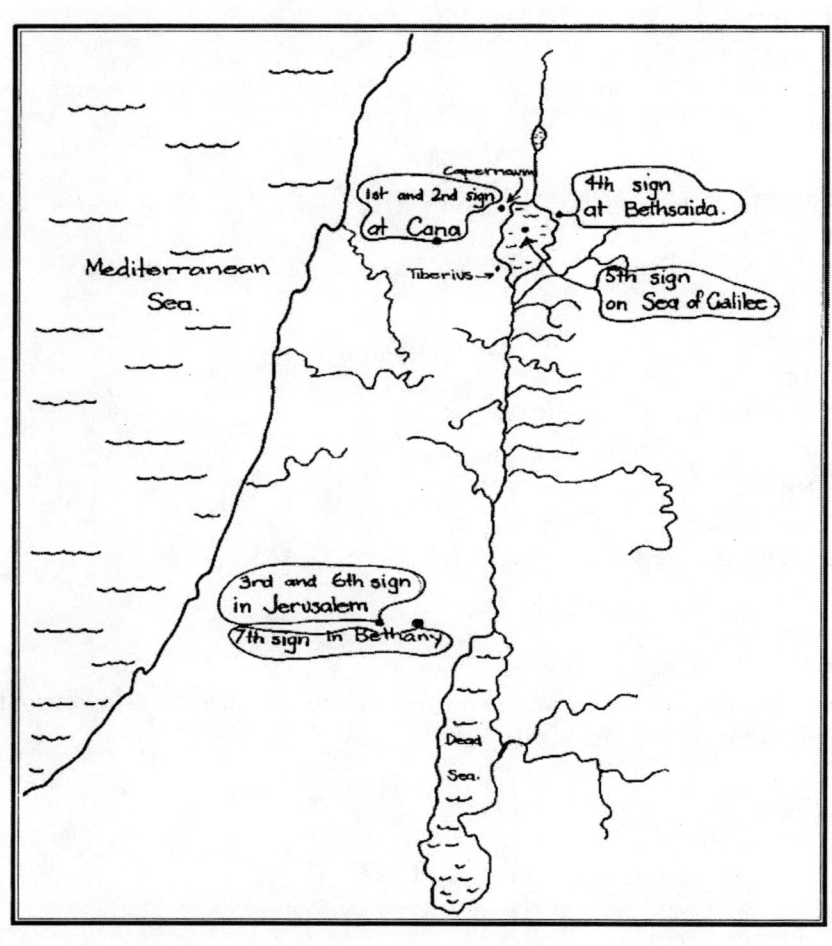

JEWISH FEASTS THAT CONNECT WITH THE SIGNS

The concurrence of the signs of Jesus i.e. the things that he did according to the Gospel of John, and which occurred at the culmination of the Jewish Liturgies, has significance. Jesus, the Jew, brought to fulfillment in himself, the Jewish feasts to tell WHO HE IS, for them and for us.

New Creation—New Wine. Jn 1:19; 2:11

John the Baptist recognised and proclaimed Jesus the Messiah, The Lamb of God promised by Abraham. Hope for the Messiah changed then to belief in Jesus by his disciples when Jesus worked his first miracle at the wedding feast at Cana, where the new Messianic age began. Jesus was determined to devote himself entirely to serve His Father.

The First Passover. Jn 2:12; 4:54

The first Passover, with accompanying events ended with the second miracle at Cana, when at the seventh hour, the Nobleman's son passed over from sickness to health and the Nobleman and his whole household passed over from unbelief to belief.

The Sabbath Feast Jn 5: 1-47

On the Sabbath Feast when at Jerusalem, Jesus cured the 'paralytic', he insisted on absolute harmony of activity between himself and his Father. This required identity of the divine nature of Jesus with his Father. We see Jesus dispensing to people life that the Father bestows through his Son.

The Feast of Passover Jn 6: 1-17. (April-Spring)

The feast of Passover commemorates the Exodus redemption and deliverance and is also known as the Feast of Unleavened Bread. In the desert Jesus multiplied five loaves to feed 5000 men. He also walked across the Sea of Galilee leading his disciples to their destination.

The Feast of Tabernacles Jn 7: 1-10, 21

The Feast of Tabernacles, or harvest, marked the end of one year and the beginning of a new one. It was at this feast in Jerusalem, that Jesus performed two miracles. He gave sight to the man who was blind since birth and also gave this man, the gift of faith in Himself as the Messiah.

The Feast of Dedication of the Temple Jn 10: 22—11:54

In past history, the Greeks had desecrated the Temple and Judas Maccabeus defeated them at war. After this, in 164 BC, the Temple was reconstructed and rededicated. It was at the end of this commemorative feast of the Dedication that Jesus raised Lazarus from the dead.

SEVEN SIGNS

A WEDDING IN CANA
JESUS REVEALED HIS GLORY

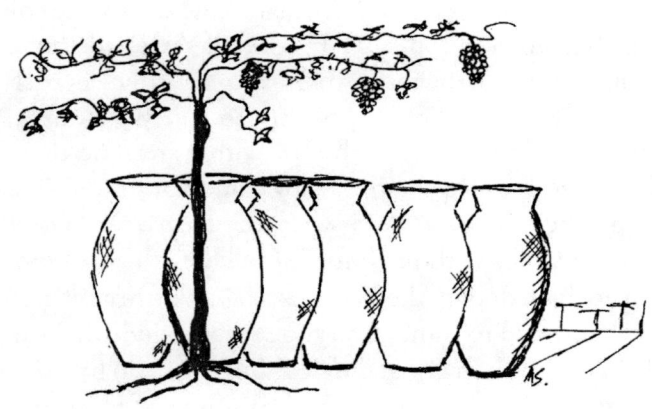

PART ONE—FIRST SIGN

Read—The wedding at Cana Jn 2:1-12
Read—Outline the narrative
Read—Highlight any significant words or phrases
Read—Observe personal responses/relationships of characters

Reflect—Listen to your felt responses.
Reflect—Insights/values clarified.

Journal—Write "in role as any chosen character"
Resolution—Affirmation/prayer or mantra
Mandala—Draw essential idea.
Notes—Any connected personal ideas

First Sign

The Wedding in Cana
Jn: 2:2-12.

Reading to establish the literal meaning using the first level of imagery, the surface or sensory level.

On the third day there was a wedding in Cana in Galilee, and the mother of Jesus was there. [2] Jesus and his disciples were also invited to the wedding. [3] When the wine ran short, the Mother of Jesus said to Him, "They have no wine." [4] And Jesus said to Her, "Woman, how does your concern affect Me? My hour has not yet come." [5] His Mother said to the servers, "Do whatever He tells you."[6] Now there were six stone water jars there for Jewish ceremonial washings, each holding twenty to thirty gallons. [91 litres to 136 litres.] [7] Jesus told them, "Fill the jars with water." So they filled them to the brim. [8] Then He told them, "Draw some out now and take it to the headwaiter." So they took it. [9] And when the headwaiter tasted the water that had become wine, without knowing where it came from (although the servers who had drawn the water knew), the headwaiter called the Bridegroom [10] and said to him, "Everyone serves good wine first, and then when people have drunk freely, an inferior one; but you have kept the good wine until now." [11] Jesus did this as the beginning of His signs in Cana in Galilee and so revealed His glory, and his disciples began to believe in Him [12] After this, he and his Mother, [his] brothers and his disciples went down to Capernaum and stayed there only a few days.

RESPONSE AT THE SENSORY LEVEL OF IMAGERY

Setting;

- Where did the event take place?
- When (historically)?
- What was the event?

Characters:

- Who are the major characters?
- Who are the minor characters?

Dilemma or human problem;

- What was the problem?
- Who was affected by the problem?

Action:

- Who initiated a response?
- How did Jesus respond to this human problem?

Conclusion;

- What were the final results for the major characters?
- What were the results for minor characters?

What do I sense from this scene?

First Sign

The Wedding in Cana
Jn: 2:2-12.

Reading to establish the *second level of imagery-the* recollective/ analytic level to evoke my personal connected memories.

On the third day there was a wedding in Cana in Galilee, and the mother of Jesus was there. ²Jesus and his disciples were also invited to the wedding. ³ When the wine ran short, the Mother of Jesus said to Him, "They have no wine." ⁴· And Jesus said to Her, "Woman, how does your concern affect Me? My hour has not yet come." ⁵· His Mother said to the servers, "Do whatever He tells you."⁶· Now there were six stone water jars there for Jewish ceremonial washings, each holding twenty to thirty gallons.[91 litres to 136 litres.] ⁷· Jesus told them, "Fill the jars with water." So they filled them to the brim. ⁸· Then He told them, "Draw some out now and take it to the headwaiter." So they took it. ⁹· And when the headwaiter tasted the water that had become wine, without knowing where it came from (although the servers who had drawn the water knew), the headwaiter called the Bridegroom ¹⁰· and said to him, "Everyone serves good wine first, and then when people have drunk freely, an inferior one; but you have kept the good wine until now." ¹¹· Jesus did this as the beginning of His signs in Cana in Galilee and so revealed His glory, and his disciples began to believe in Him ¹²· After this, he and his Mother, [his] brothers and his disciples went down to Capernaum and stayed there only a few days.

RESPONSE AT THE RECOLLECTIVE—ANALYTIC LEVEL OF IMAGERY.

Here I study my own past, my problems and my potentialities. Memories both verbal and visual are accessed as I analyse this narrative. I resonate parallels in my own life.

Narrative Structure: Diagram

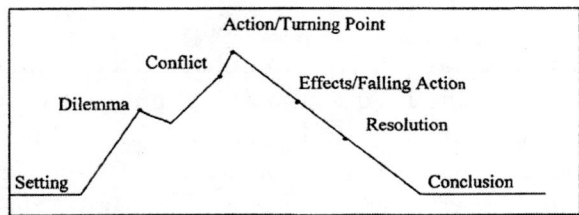

Setting:
- I transport myself imaginally to the place. _____
- I connect with a character of my choice viz _____

Characters—
- I empathise with a certain person viz _____
  or persons viz _____
  _____

The dilemma/human problem;
- I accept this as my own problem.
- I experience the suffering.
- I take on board the needs.

Action—
- I recognize my own potential to solve problems, to be proactive and to decide in favour of goal setting and positive intention to act.

Conclusion
- What are the final results for me from my identification with my chosen character?

What have I become more aware of?
- What message have I found in this scene that connects with memories in my own life experience?

First Sign

The Wedding in Cana
Jn: 2:2-12.

Reading to establish the *third level of imagery*, the symbolic level. This enables me to connect with mythical and archetypal figures. Here I find that symbols can have relevance to my life.

On the third day there was a wedding in Cana in Galilee, and the mother of Jesus was there. ² Jesus and his disciples were also invited to the wedding. ³ When the wine ran short, the Mother of Jesus said to Him, "They have no wine." ⁴· And Jesus said to Her, "Woman, how does your concern affect Me? My hour has not yet come." ⁵· His Mother said to the servers, "Do whatever He tells you."⁶· Now there were six stone water jars there for Jewish ceremonial washings, each holding twenty to thirty gallons.[91 litres to 136 litres.] ⁷· Jesus told them, "Fill the jars with water." So they filled them to the brim. $. Then He told them, "Draw some out now and take it to the headwaiter." So they took it. ⁵· And when the headwaiter tasted the water that had become wine, without knowing where it came from (although the servers who had drawn the water knew), the headwaiter called the Bridegroom ¹⁰· and said to him, "Everyone serves good wine first, and then when people have drunk freely, an inferior one; but you have kept the good wine until now." it. Jesus did this as the beginning of His signs in Cana in Galilee and so revealed His glory, and his disciples began to believe in Him ¹²· After this, he and his Mother, [his] brothers and his disciples went down to Capernaum and stayed there only a few days.

Seven Signs

RESPONSE AT THE SYMBOLIC LEVEL OF IMAGERY

I highlight words or phrases that symbolize and reflect patterns in my own personal life and its context. These symbolic images move me beyond my own personal-particular, toward more universal formulations. Here I'm able to experience a sense of continuity with evolutionary and historic process. I may identify with archetypical figures that have relevance to my own life and to my own problems.

Rational evaluation:

- I "become" this archetypal character to experience the facts of the situation, the values and relationship between this person and Jesus.
- I transfer this imaginal experience to my own real life situation.
- I observe the responsive action of Jesus toward _____
- I identify with the feelings of this character toward Jesus _____
- I observe the actions of other major characters _____
- I identify with the feelings of Jesus to this person _____
- I too participate in the feelings, needs and responses of the characters with whom I have chosen to identify.

The feelings and needs of the characters were connected, so that a final result occurred at that time and in that place.

From this consideration I choose a symbol that has power to recall for me the images that are now imprinted in my senses, in my memory and in my experience.

> I draw and label my chosen symbol.

The symbols I've selected have relevance to my own life as they represent my connection with my consciousness of sources of deep knowing and the reality of creative processes

First Sign

The Wedding in Cana
Jn: 2:2-12.

Reading to establish *the fourth level of imagery*, the integral level of my own experience. Here I find my own essence or "groundedness." I find a sense of new commitment to and communion with social, ecological and spiritual order. I gaze at the scene with love and become open to an awareness of order and presence.

On the third day there was a wedding in Cana in Galilee, and the mother of Jesus was there. ² Jesus and his disciples were also invited to the wedding. ³ When the wine ran short, the Mother of Jesus said to Him, "They have no wine." ⁴· And Jesus said to Her, "Woman, how does your concern affect Me? My hour has not yet come." ⁵· His Mother said to the servers, "Do whatever He tells you."⁶· Now there were six stone water jars there for Jewish ceremonial washings, each holding twenty to thirty gallons.[91 litres to 136 litres.] ⁷· Jesus told them, "Fill the jars with water." So they filled them to the brim. 8. Then He told them, "Draw some out now and take it to the headwaiter." So they took it. ⁹· And when the headwaiter tasted the water that had become wine, without knowing where it came from (although the servers who had drawn the water knew), the headwaiter called the Bridegroom lo. and said to him, "Everyone serves good wine first, and then when people have drunk freely, an inferior one; but you have kept the good wine until now." ¹¹· Jesus did this as the beginning of His signs in Cana in Galilee and so revealed His glory, and his disciples began to believe in Him ¹²· After this, he and his Mother, [his] brothers and his disciples went down to Capernaum and stayed there only a few days.

RESPONSE AT THE INTEGRAL LEVEL OF IMAGERY

Herein I descend to a level of awareness in which I experience my own true essence or the 'Ground of my Being'. Here I'm enabled to find The Holy Grail', the cornucopia, and to courageously "launch out into the deep". I experience that the universe outside is reflected on the inside and I find that Great Nature is contained within both. Images and archetypes can become for me structural forms that mirror to me, the wider reality of the energy of life. Persons portrayed in this human event experienced a new sightedness.

> In the light of the life, death and resurrection of Jesus—what does this text say to me?

I become aware of possibilities of involvement in deep contemplation, in works of compassion, of hospitality and generosity in response to the Risen Presence and power of that which the renowned Tielhard de Chardin called "The Within".

I pray for the grace to wholeheartedly respond to that Echo within. Those things that I have sensed, recalled and identified with, connect with a still point and are accessed through this SIGN.

> What do I say to JESUS who speaks to me in this text?

Seven Signs

Reflection to listen.

I **listen** to 'felt' responses to the issues that this story encourages in me to effect **action.**

What is it that I yearn to move toward?

What does the Spirit of Jesus want me to do today?

Why did the 'Holy Spirit choose this **event** to effect an ACTION of Jesus?

I LISTEN to my heart, the core of my being, where the Holy Spirit moves and I speak to Jesus about any things that connect me with this Sign of Jesus.

I record the words, images or feelings that connect me with the compassionate feelings and actions of Jesus.

Words ↓	*Feelings* ↓	*Images* ↓

Seven Signs

Reflection for insight.

I have some insights regarding my own values and attitudes that compare with the attitudes of compassion, hospitality and inclusion of Jesus toward persons present in this event.

I have become aware that He has the desire and power to help me to improve or to develop my personal relationships with my family, my friends and with Him from the following:

A WORD from scripture	A value that Jesus exhibits
Some unique relationship that Jesus communicates.	Some personal enlightenment

Seven Signs

I reflect on the **values** that the characters portray for **insight** to clarify my own values.

Which characters?	What values do they exhibit?
_____	_____
_____	_____
_____	_____
_____	_____

I choose to 'step' into the persona or character of_____ with whom I empathise to become conscious that . . .

I too am called to:

- a new awareness
  e.g. _____
  _____

- a new
  perception _____
  _____

- a new enlightenment
  concerning _____
  _____

- a new application ie, action
  _____
  _____

Seven Signs

Some suggestions to **journal** my response to this Sign of Jesus.

Identification with the persona—

- I "become" one of the characters in this event and write "in role" from their perspective or perspectives.

I write—(of what happened in heart today when I met Jesus in this event).

- a letter to God, to Mary, or to my own inner spirit.
- a poem, prayer or lyric.
- about my reactions to any specific character.

I identify—

- the people I celebrate who are in my life.
- what I celebrate in my own life.
- my own differences.
- my own uniqueness.
- my own gifts, talents and capabilities.

I construct—

- what the symbols in this scene resemble or mean for me. (e.g. empty jars, wine, bread)
- a crossword puzzle with both questions and answers.

I draw—

- symbols that I've identified as having meaning that connect me with this Sign.

THE WEDDING AT CANA

Seven Signs

Journal in response to a "Wedding in Cana" Date: / /

Seven Signs

Resolution:

I make a resolution in response to my reflection on the Wedding feast in Cana

I set goals for myself; long term, short term and daily goals.

	Long term goal	Short term goal	Daily goal
What is the goal?			
Why?			
Time frame of realising this goal			
I visualise myself achieving my goals and draw this.			

I make a personal affirmation _____

I isolate a mantra from the reading _____

Seven Signs

Wedding in Cana
Mandala

I may have become aware of a central and powerful meaning from focusing on this event.

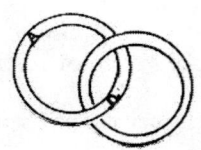

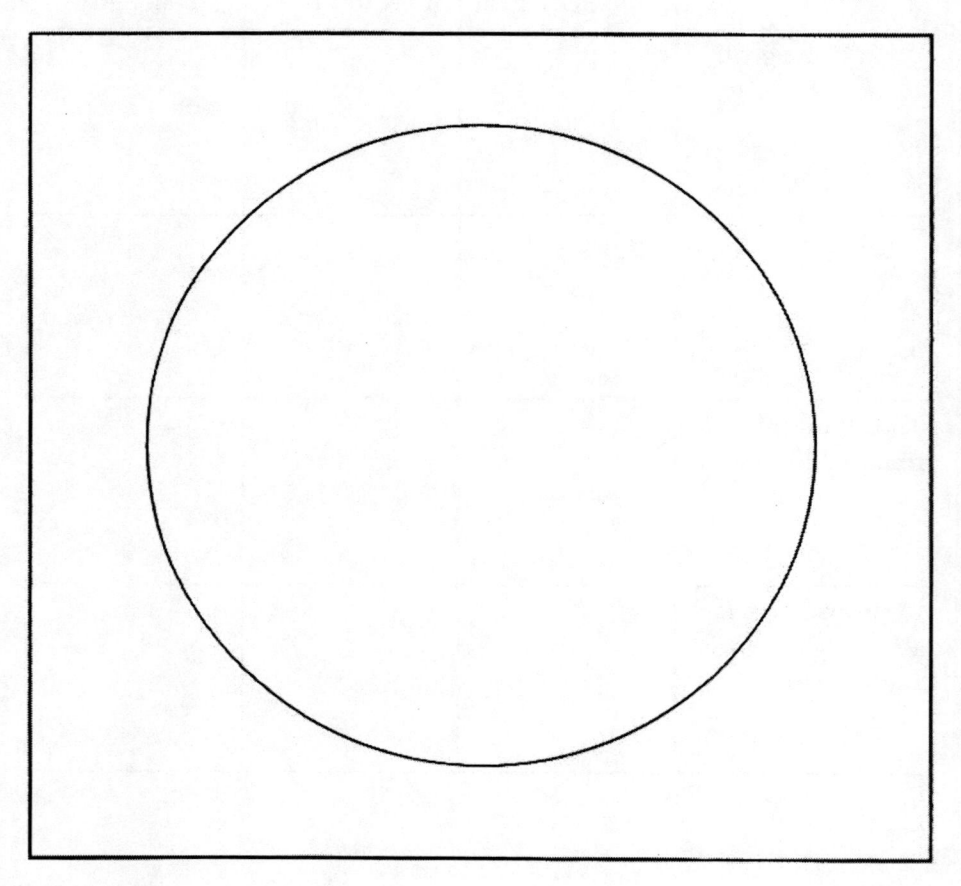

Perhaps to draw a meaningful symbol (that typifies, represents or recalls some idea or quality), within the mandala may register for me the power I've derived from considering or contemplating this sign.

SEVEN SIGNS OF ST. JOHN

Seven Signs

Recapitulation or Examine.

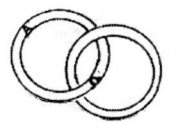

From reading about and contemplating the actions and attitudes of Jesus in this significant event, I have realised an aspect of the true nature and identity of Jesus-viz _____

This realisation has the power to call me to respond using the four functions of my psyche, to sense, to think, to feel emotionally and to use my intuition. It is this last function of intuition that *connects* me with the *risen presence of Jesus,* transferred to me in this event and that invites me to grow in love, patience, kindness and service toward my family and also within my social and professional world.

I visualise myself engaged in a particular situation where I am empowered to pray, to act with hospitality, compassion or patience in response to the persons whom I encounter in my life today. I draw this mental projection of myself acting positively, within the circular diagram.

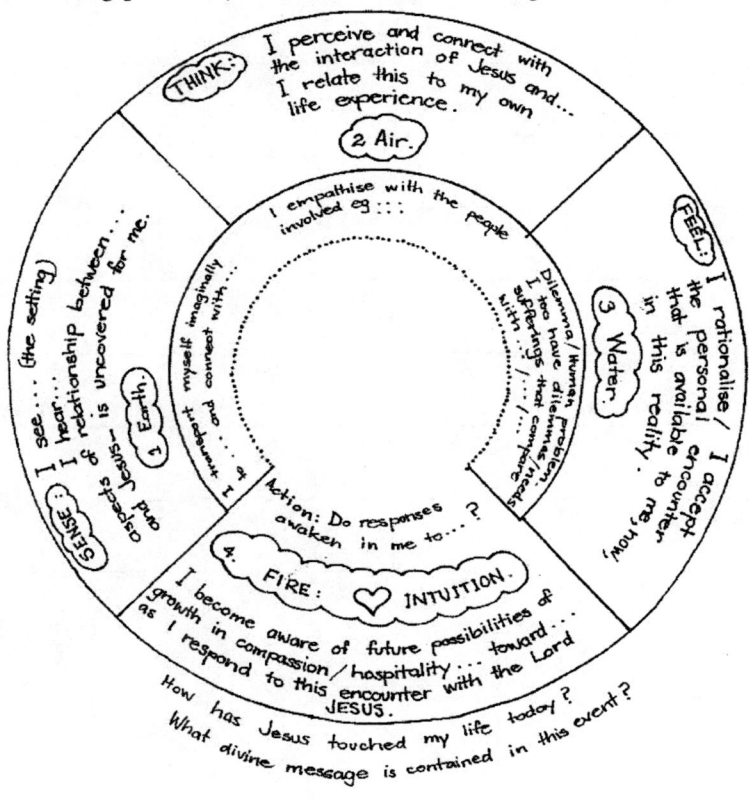

THINK: I perceive and connect with the interaction of Jesus and... I relate this to my own life experience.

2 Air.

I empathise with the people involved eg :::

FEEL: I rationalise / I accept the personal encounter that is available to me in this reality now.

3 Water.

Dilemma / Human problem / I too have dilemmas / sufferings that compare with...

SENSE: I see... I hear... (the setting) aspects of relationship between... of Jesus is uncovered for me.

1 Earth.

I project myself imaginally and connect with...

Action: Do responses awaken in me to...?

4. FIRE: ♡ INTUITION.

I become aware of future possibilities of growth in compassion / hospitality... toward... as I respond to this encounter with the Lord JESUS.

How has Jesus touched my life today?
What divine message is contained in this event?

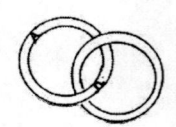

NOTES

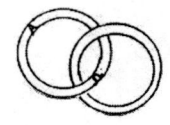

NOTES

SEVEN SIGNS

CURE OF THE NOBLEMAN'S SON
JESUS HEALED FROM A DISTANCE

Cana

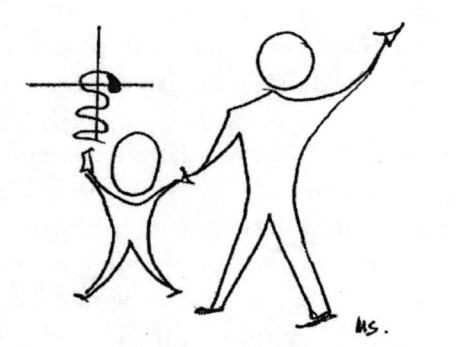

Capernaum.

PART TWO—SECOND SIGN

Read—The cure of the nobleman's son Jn 4:43-54
Read—Outline the narrative
Read—Highlight any significant words or phrases
Read—Observe personal responses/relationships of characters

Reflect—Listen to your felt responses.
Reflect—Insights/values clarified.

Journal—Write "in role as any chosen character"
Resolution—Affirmation/prayer or mantra
Mandala—Draw essential idea.
Notes—Any connected personal ideas

Second Sign

The Cure of the Nobleman's Son.
Jn:4: 43-54

Reading to establish the literal meaning using the first level of imagery, the surface or sensory level.

Return to Galilee. ⁴³ * After the two days, he left there for Galilee. ⁴⁴ For Jesus himself testified that a prophet has no honour in his native place. ⁴⁵ When he came into Galilee, the Galileans welcomed him, since they had seen all he had done in Jerusalem at the feast; for they themselves had gone to the feast.

Second Sign at Cana. ⁴⁶ Then he returned to Cana in Galilee, where he had made water wine. Now there was a royal official whose son was ill in Capernaum. ⁴⁷ When he heard that Jesus had arrived in Galilee from Judea, he went to him and asked him to come down and heal his son, who was near death. ⁴⁸ Jesus said to him, "Unless you people see signs and wonders, you will not believe."⁴⁹ The royal official said to him, "Sir, come down before my child dies." ⁵⁰ Jesus said to him, "You may go; your son will live." The man believed what Jesus said to him and left. ⁵¹ While he was on his way back, his slaves met him and told him that his boy would live. ⁵² He asked them when he began to recover. They told him, "The fever left him yesterday, about one in the afternoon." ⁵³ The father realised that just at the time that Jesus had said to him, "Your son will live," and he and his whole household came to believe. ⁵⁴ [Now] this was the second sign Jesus did when he came to Galilee from Judea.

RESPONSE AT THE SENSORY LEVEL OF IMAGERY

Setting:

- Where did the event take place?
- When (historically)?
- What was the event?

Characters;

- Who are the major characters?
- Who are the minor characters?

Dilemma or human problem;

- What was the problem?
- Who was affected by the problem?

Act on-

- Who initiated a response?
- How did Jesus respond to this human problem?

Conclusion;

- What were the final results for the major characters?
- What were the results for minor characters?

What do I sense from this scene?

Second Sign

The Cure of the Nobleman's Son.
Jn:4: 43-54

Reading to establish the *second level of imagery*, the recollective/analytic level to evoke personal connected memories.

Return to Galilee. [43] * After the two days, he left there for Galilee. [44] For Jesus himself testified that a prophet has no honour in his native place. [45] When he came into Galilee, the Galileans welcomed him, since they had seen all he had done in Jerusalem at the feast; for they themselves had gone to the feast.

Second Sign at Cana. [46] Then he returned to Cana in Galilee, where he had made water wine. Now there was a royal official whose son was ill in Capernaum. [47] When he heard that Jesus had arrived in Galilee from Judea, he went to him and asked him to come down and heal his son, who was near death. [48] Jesus said to him, "Unless you people see signs and wonders, you will not believe." [49] The royal official said to him, "Sir, come down before my child dies." [50] Jesus said to him, "You may go; your son will live." The man believed what Jesus said to him and left. [51] While he was on his way back, his slaves met him and told him that his boy would live. [52] He asked them when he began to recover. They told him, "The fever left him yesterday, about one in the afternoon." [53] The father realised that just at the time that Jesus had said to him, "Your son will live," and he and his whole household came to believe. [54] [Now] this was the second sign Jesus did when he came to Galilee from Judea.

RESPONSE AT THE RECOLLECTIVE—ANALYTIC LEVEL OF IMAGERY.

Here I study my own past, my problems and my potentialities. Memories both verbal and visual are accessed as I analyse this narrative. I resonate parallels in my own life.

Narrative Structure: Diagram

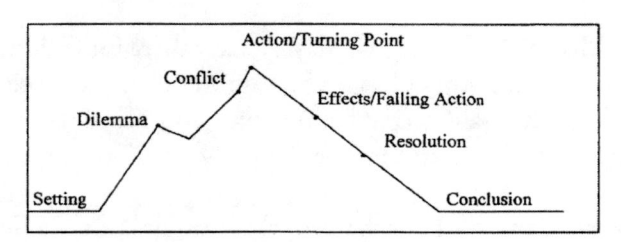

Setting:
- I transport myself imaginally to the place. _____
- I connect with a character of my choice viz _____

Characters—
- I empathise with a certain person viz _____
  or persons viz _____
  _____

The dilemma/human problem;
- I accept this as my own problem.
- I experience the suffering.
- I take on board the needs.

Action—
- I recognize my own potential to solve problems, to be proactive and to decide in favour of goal setting and positive intention to act.

Conclusion
- What are the final results for me from my identification with my chosen character?

What have I become more aware of?
- What message have I found in this scene that connects with memories in my own life experience?

Second Sign

The Cure of the Nobleman's Son.
Jn:4: 43-54

Reading to establish the *third level of imagery,* the symbolic level. This enables me to connect with mythical and archetypal figures. Here I find that symbols can have relevance to my life.

Return to Galilee. [43] * After the two days, he left there for Galilee. [44] For Jesus himself testified that a prophet has no honour in his native place. [45] When he came into Galilee, the Galileans welcomed him, since they had seen all he had done in Jerusalem at the feast; for they themselves had gone to the feast.

Second Sign at Cana. [46] Then he returned to Cana in Galilee, where he had made water wine. Now there was a royal official whose son was ill in Capernaum. [47] When he heard that Jesus had arrived in Galilee from Judea, he went to him and asked him to come down and heal his son, who was near death. [48] Jesus said to him, "Unless you people see signs and wonders, you will not believe."[49] The royal official said to him, "Sir, come down before my child dies." [50] Jesus said to him, "You may go; your son will live." The man believed what Jesus said to him and left. [51] While he was on his way back, his slaves met him and told him that his boy would live. [52] He asked them when he began to recover. They told him, "The fever left him yesterday, about one in the afternoon." [53] The father realised that just at the time that Jesus had said to him, "Your son will live," and he and his whole household came to believe. [54] [Now] this was the second sign Jesus did when he came to Galilee from Judea.

RESPONSE AT THE SYMBOLIC LEVEL OF IMAGERY

I highlight words or phrases that symbolize and reflect patterns in my own personal life and its context. These symbolic images move me beyond my own personal-particular, toward more universal formulations. Here I'm able to experience a sense of continuity with evolutionary and historic process. I may identify with archetypical figures that have relevance to my own life and to my own problems.

Rational evaluation:

- I "become" this archetypal character to experience the facts of the situation, the values and relationship between this person and Jesus.
- I transfer this imaginal experience to my own real life situation.
- I observe the responsive action of Jesus toward _____
- I identify with the feelings of this character toward Jesus _____
- I observe the actions of other major characters _____
- I identify with the feelings of Jesus to this person _____
- I too participate in the feelings, needs and responses of the characters with whom I have chosen to identify.

The feelings and needs of the characters were connected, so that a final result occurred at that time and in that place.

From this consideration I choose a symbol that has power to recall for me the images that are now imprinted in my senses, in my memory and in my experience.

I draw and label my chosen symbol.

The symbols I've selected have relevance to my own life as they represent my connection with my consciousness of sources of deep knowing and the reality of creative processes

Second Sign

The Cure of the Nobleman's Son.
Jn:4: 43-54

Reading to establish *the fourth level of imagery*, the integral level of my own experience. Here I find my own essence or "groundedness." I find a sense of new commitment to and communion with social, ecological and spiritual order. I gaze at the scene with love and become open to an awareness of order and presence.

Return to Galilee. [43] * After the two days, he left there for Galilee. [44] For Jesus himself testified that a prophet has no honour in his native place. [45] When he came into Galilee, the Galileans welcomed him, since they had seen all he had done in Jerusalem at the feast; for they themselves had gone to the feast.

Second Sign at Cana. [46] Then he returned to Cana in Galilee, where he had made water wine. Now there was a royal official whose son was ill in Capernaum. [47] When he heard that Jesus had arrived in Galilee from Judea, he went to him and asked him to come down and heal his son, who was near death. [48] Jesus said to him, "Unless you people see signs and wonders, you will not believe."[49] The royal official said to him, "Sir, come down before my child dies." [50] Jesus said to him, "You may go; your son will live." The man believed what Jesus said to him and left. [51] While he was on his way back, his slaves met him and told him that his boy would live. [52] He asked them when he began to recover. They told him, "The fever left him yesterday, about one in the afternoon." [53] The father realised that just at the time that Jesus had said to him, "Your son will live," and he and his whole household came to believe. [54] [Now] this was the second sign Jesus did when he came to Galilee from Judea.

Seven Signs

RESPONSE AT THE INTEGRAL LEVEL OF IMAGERY

Herein I descend to a level of awareness in which I experience my own true essence or the 'Ground of my Being'. Here I'm enabled to find The Holy Grail', the Cornucopia, and to courageously "launch out into the deep". I experience that the universe outside, is reflected on the inside, and I find that Great Nature is contained within both. Images and archetypes can become for me structural forms that mirror to me, the wider reality of the energy of life. Persons portrayed in this human event experienced a new sightedness.

> In the light of the life, death and resurrection of Jesus, what does this text say to me?

I become aware of possibilities of involvement in deep contemplation, in works of compassion, of hospitality and generosity in response to the Risen Presence and power of that which the renowned Tielhard de Chardin called "The Within".

I pray for the grace to wholeheartedly respond to that Echo within. Those things that I have sensed, recalled and identified with, connect with a still point and are accessed through this SIGN.

> What do I say to JESUS who speaks to me in this text?

Seven Signs

Reflection to listen.

I **listen** to 'felt' responses to the issues that this story encourages in me to effect **action**.

What is it that I yearn to move toward?

What does the Spirit of Jesus want me to do today?

Why did the 'Holy Spirit choose this **event** to effect an ACTION of Jesus?

I LISTEN to my heart, the core of my being, where the Holy Spirit moves and I speak to Jesus about any things that connect me with this Sign of Jesus.

I record the words, images or feelings that connect me with the compassionate feelings and actions of Jesus.

Words	*Feelings*	*Images*
↓	↓	↓

Seven Signs

Reflection for insight.

I have some insights regarding my own values and attitudes that compare with the attitudes of compassion, hospitality and inclusion of Jesus toward persons present in this event.

I have become aware that He has the desire and power to help me to improve or to develop my personal relationships with my family, my friends and with Him from the following:

A WORD from scripture	A value that Jesus exhibits
Some unique relationship that Jesus communicates.	Some personal enlightenment

Seven Signs

I reflect on the **values** that the characters portray for **insight** to clarify my own values.

Which characters?	What values do they exhibit?
_____	_____
_____	_____
_____	_____
_____	_____

I choose to 'step' into the persona or character of_____
with whom I empathise to become conscious that . . .

I too am called to:

- a new awareness
  e.g. _____
  _____

- a new
  perception _____
  _____

- a new enlightenment
  concerning _____
  _____

- a new application ie, action
  _____

Seven Signs

Some suggestions to **journal** my response to this Sign of Jesus.

Identification with the persona—

- I "become" one of the characters in this event and write "in role" from their perspective or perspectives.

I write—(of what happened in heart today when I met Jesus in this event).

- a letter to God, to Mary, or to my own inner spirit.
- a poem, prayer or lyric.
- about my reactions to any specific character.

I identify—

- the people I celebrate who are in my life.
- what I celebrate in my own life.
- my own differences.
- my own uniqueness.
- my own gifts, talents and capabilities.

I construct—

- what the symbols in this scene resemble or mean for me. (e.g. empty jars, wine, bread)
- a crossword puzzle with both questions and answers.

I draw—

- symbols that I've identified as having meaning that connect me with this Sign.

Seven Signs

Journal in response to the cure of the Nobleman's son   Date: / /

_____

_____

_____

_____

_____

_____

_____

_____

_____

_____

_____

_____

_____

_____

Seven Signs

Resolution

I ask for the grace to respond enthusiastically to the revelation I have received in this reflection on God's love, His intimacy and His power. I ask that God's name will be honoured and that God's reign will be achieved in me and in all people everywhere, as I make my resolutions.

	Long term goal	Short term goal	Daily goal
What is the goal?			
Why?			
Time frame of realising this goal			
I visualise myself achieving my goals and draw this.			

I make a personal affirmation _____

I isolate a mantra from the reading _____

Seven Signs

Cure of Nobleman's Son
Mandala

I may have become aware of a central and powerful meaning from focusing on this event.

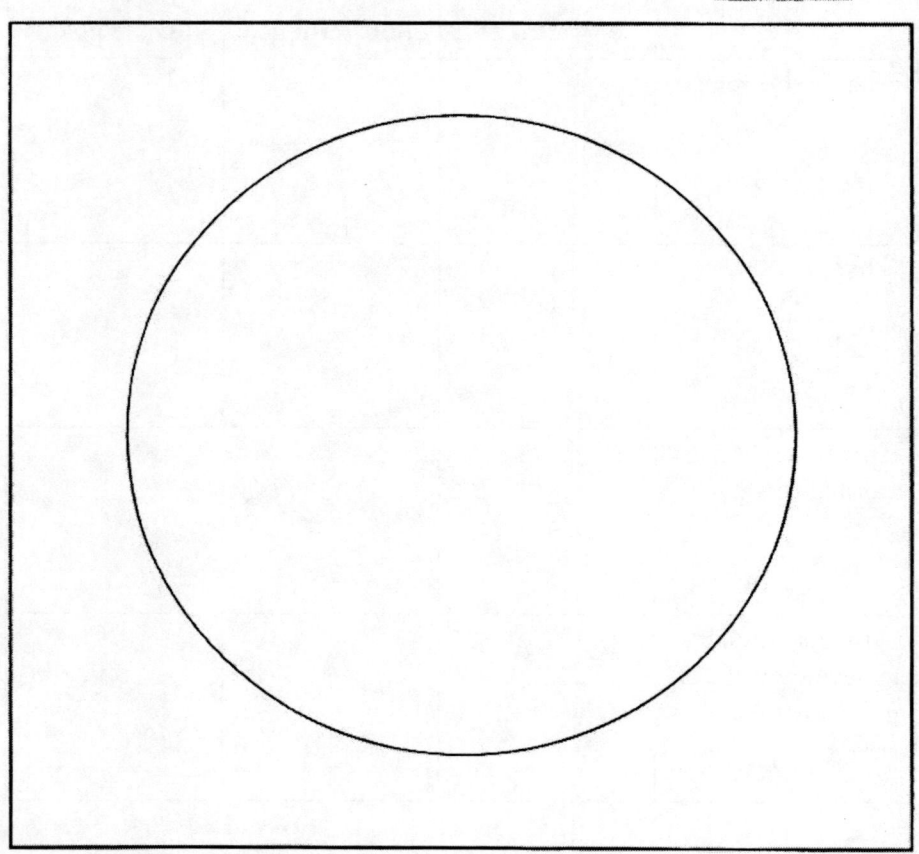

Perhaps to draw a meaningful symbol (that typifies, represents or recalls some idea or quality), within the mandala may register for me the power I've derived from considering or contemplating this sign.

Seven Signs

Recapitulation or Examine.

From reading about and contemplating the actions and attitudes of Jesus in this significant event, I have realised an aspect of the true nature and identity of Jesus-viz _____

This realisation has the power to call me to respond using the four functions of my psyche, to sense, to think, to feel emotionally and to use my intuition. It is this last function of intuition that *connects* me with the *risen presence of Jesus,* transferred to me in this event and that invites me to grow in love, patience, kindness and service toward my family and also within my social and professional world.

I visualise myself engaged in a particular situation where I am empowered to pray, to act with hospitality, compassion or patience in response to the persons whom I encounter in my life today. I draw this mental projection of myself acting positively, within the circular diagram.

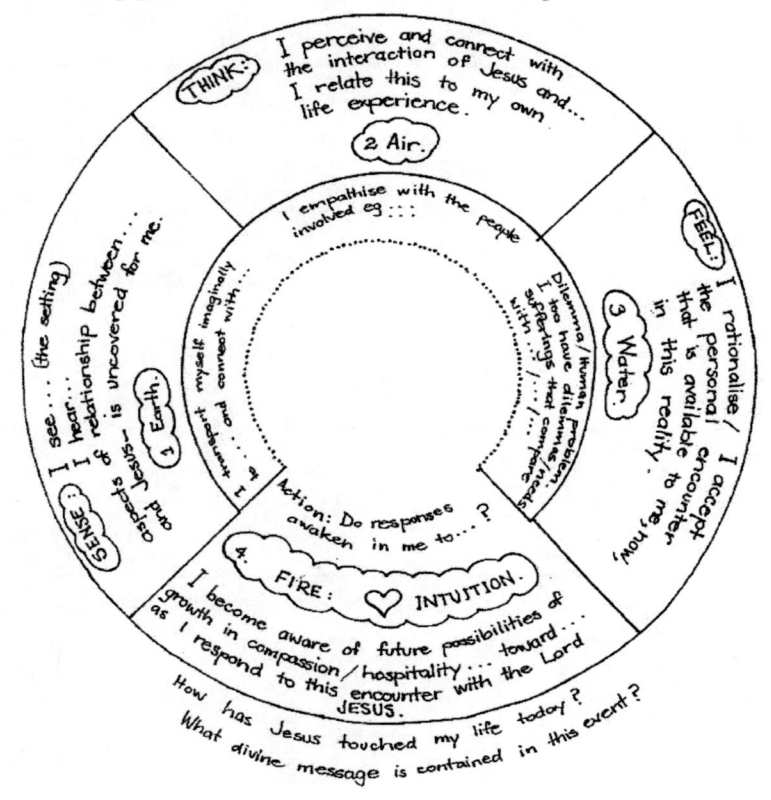

Diagram: A circular diagram divided into four quadrants labelled with the four functions and elements:

- **THINK / 2. Air:** I perceive and connect with the interaction of Jesus and... I relate this to my own life experience.
- **FEEL / 3. Water:** I rationalise / I accept the personal encounter that is available to me in this reality, now.
- **SENSE / 1. Earth:** I see... I hear... (the setting) and relationship between... aspects of Jesus is uncovered for me.
- **FIRE / 4. INTUITION:** I become aware of future possibilities of growth in compassion / hospitality... as I respond to this encounter with the Lord JESUS. How has Jesus touched my life today? What divine message is contained in this event?

Inner ring: I empathise with the people involved eg :::... Dilemma / Human problem / suffering that connected with... I support myself imaginally and connect with...

Centre: Action: Do responses awaken in me to...?

NOTES

NOTES

SEVEN SIGNS

CURE OF THE PARALYTIC AT BETHESDA
A HEALING

PART THREE—THIRD SIGN

Read—The cure of the paralysed man at the 'Sheep Pool' (Jerusalem) Jn 5:1-9
Read—Outline the narrative
Read—Highlight any significant words or phrases
Read—Observe personal responses/relationships of characters

Reflect—Listen to your felt responses.
Reflect—Insights/values clarified.

Journal—Write "in role as any chosen character"
Resolution—Affirmation/prayer or mantra
Mandala—Draw essential idea.
Notes—Any connected personal ideas

Third Sign:

**The cure of the man at the Sheep Pool on the Sabbath.
Jn 5: 1-9**

Reading to establish the literal meaning using the first level of imagery, the surface or sensory level.

After this, there was a feast of the Jews, and Jesus went up to Jerusalem. ² Now there is in Jerusalem at the Sheep [Gate] a pool called in Hebrew Bethesda, with five porticoes. ³ In these there lay a large number of ill, blind, lame, and crippled. [4*] ⁵ One man was there who had been ill for thirty eight years. ⁶ When Jesus saw him lying there and knew that he had been ill for a long time, he said to him

"Do you want to be well?" ⁷ The sick man answered him, "Sir I have no one to put me into the pool where the water is stirred up; while I am on my way, someone else gets down there before me."

⁸ Jesus said to him, "Rise, take up your mat, and walk." ⁹ Immediately the man became well, took up his mat, and walked. Now that day was a Sabbath.

[Note—Feasts of both "Passover" and Tabernacles" were referred to by the Jews as "THE FEAST"]

RESPONSE AT THE SENSORY LEVEL OF IMAGERY

Setting:.

- Where did the event take place?
- When (historically)?
- What was the event?

Characters;

- Who are the major characters?
- Who are the minor characters?

Dilemma or human problem;

- What was the problem?
- Who was affected by the problem?

Action.

- Who initiated a response?
- How did Jesus respond to this human problem?

Conclusion:

- What were the final results for the major characters?
- What were the results for minor characters?

What do I sense from this scene?

Third Sign:

**The cure of the man at the Sheep Pool on the Sabbath.
Jn 5: 1-9**

Reading to establish the *second level of imagery*, the recollective/analytic level to evoke personal connected memories.

After this, there was a feast of the Jews, and Jesus went up to Jerusalem. ² Now there is in Jerusalem at the Sheep [Gate] a pool called in Hebrew Bethesda, with five porticoes. ³ In these there lay a large number of ill, blind, lame, and crippled. [4*] ⁵ One man was there who had been ill for thirty eight years. ⁶ When Jesus saw him lying there and knew that he had been ill for a long time, he said to him

"Do you want to be well?" ⁷ The sick man answered him, "Sir I have no one to put me into the pool where the water is stirred up; while I am on my way, someone else gets down there before me."

⁸ Jesus said to him, "Rise, take up your mat, and walk." ⁹ Immediately the man became well, took up his mat, and walked. Now that day was a Sabbath.

[Note—Feasts of both "Passover" and Tabernacles" were referred to by the Jews as "THE FEAST"]

RESPONSE AT THE RECOLLECTIVE—ANALYTIC LEVEL OF IMAGERY.

Here I study my own past, my problems and my potentialities. Memories both verbal and visual are accessed as I analyse this narrative. I resonate parallels in my own life.

Narrative Structure: Diagram

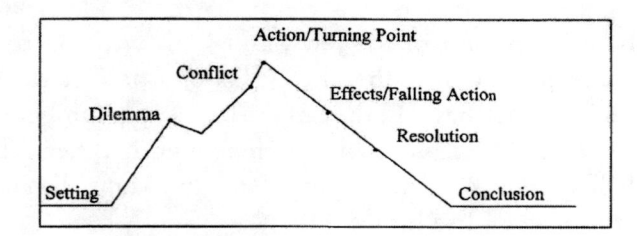

Setting:
- I transport myself imaginally to the place. _____
- I connect with a character of my choice viz _____

Characters—
- I empathise with a certain person viz _____
  or persons viz _____
  _____

The dilemma/human problem;
- I accept this as my own problem.
- I experience the suffering.
- I take on board the needs.

Action—
- I recognize my own potential to solve problems, to be proactive and to decide in favour of goal setting and positive intention to act.

Conclusion
- What are the final results for me from my identification with my chosen character?

What have I become more aware of?
- What message have I found in this scene that connects with memories in my own life experience?

Third Sign:

The cure of the man at the Sheep Pool on the Sabbath.
Jn 5: 1-9

Reading to establish the *third level of imagery*, the symbolic level. This enables me to connect with mythical and archetypal figures. Here I find that symbols can have relevance to my life.

After this, there was a feast of the Jews, and Jesus went up to Jerusalem. ² Now there is in Jerusalem at the Sheep [Gate] a pool called in Hebrew Bethesda, with five porticoes. ³ In these there lay a large number of ill, blind, lame, and crippled. [4*] ⁵ One man was there who had been ill for thirty eight years. ⁶ When Jesus saw him lying there and knew that he had been ill for a long time, he said to him

"Do you want to be well?" ⁷ The sick man answered him, "Sir I have no one to put me into the pool where the water is stirred up; while I am on my way, someone else gets down there before me."

⁸ Jesus said to him, "Rise, take up your mat, and walk." ⁹ Immediately the man became well, took up his mat, and walked. Now that day was a Sabbath.

[Note—Feasts of both "Passover" and Tabernacles" were referred to by the Jews as "THE FEAST"]

Seven Signs

RESPONSE AT THE SYMBOLIC LEVEL OF IMAGERY

I highlight words or phrases that symbolize and reflect patterns in my own personal life and its context. These symbolic images move me beyond my own personal-particular, toward more universal formulations. Here I'm able to experience a sense of continuity with evolutionary and historic process. I may identify with archetypical figures that have relevance to my own life and to my own problems.

Rational evaluation:

- I "become" this archetypal character to experience the facts of the situation, the values and relationship between this person and Jesus.
- I transfer this imaginal experience to my own real life situation.
- I observe the responsive action of Jesus toward _____
- I identify with the feelings of this character toward Jesus _____
- I observe the actions of other major characters _____
- I identify with the feelings of Jesus to this person _____
- I too participate in the feelings, needs and responses of the characters with whom I have chosen to identify.

The feelings and needs of the characters were connected, so that a final result occurred at that time and in that place.

From this consideration I choose a symbol that has power to recall for me the images that are now imprinted in my senses, in my memory and in my experience.

I draw and label my chosen symbol.

The symbols I've selected have relevance to my own life as they represent my connection with my consciousness of sources of deep knowing and the reality of creative processes

Third Sign:

**The cure of the man at the Sheep Pool on the Sabbath.
Jn 5: 1-9**

Reading to establish *the fourth level of imagery,* the integral level of my own experience. Here I find my own essence or "groundedness." I find a sense of new commitment to and communion with social, ecological and spiritual order. I gaze at the scene with love and become open to an awareness of order and presence.

¹ After this, there was a feast of the Jews, and Jesus went up to Jerusalem. ² Now there is in Jerusalem at the Sheep [Gate] a pool called in Hebrew Bethesda, with five porticoes. ³ In these there lay a large number of ill, blind, lame, and crippled. [4*] ⁵ One man was there who had been ill for thirty eight years. ⁶ When Jesus saw him lying there and knew that he had been ill for a long time, he said to him

"Do you want to be well?" ⁷ The sick man answered him, "Sir I have no one to put me into the pool where the water is stirred up; while I am on my way, someone else gets down there before me."

⁸ Jesus said to him, "Rise, take up your mat, and walk." ⁹ Immediately the man became well, took up his mat, and walked. Now that day was a Sabbath.

[Note—Feasts of both "Passover" and Tabernacles" were referred to by the Jews as "THE FEAST"]

Jn 5,4—This verse is missing from all early manuscripts and the earliest versions, including the Vulgate. Its vocabulary is markedly non-Johannine.

p1143, The New American Bible.

Seven Signs

RESPONSE AT THE INTEGRAL LEVEL OF IMAGERY

Herein I descend to a level of awareness in which I experience my own true essence or the 'Ground of my Being'. Here I'm enabled to find The Holy Grail', the Cornucopia, and to courageously "launch out into the deep". I experience that the universe outside, is reflected on the inside, and I find that Great Nature is contained within both. Images and archetypes can become for me structural forms that mirror to me, the wider reality of the energy of life. Persons portrayed in this human event experienced a new sightedness.

> In the light of the life, death and resurrection of Jesus, what does this text say to me?

I become aware of possibilities of involvement in deep contemplation, in works of compassion, of hospitality and generosity in response to the Risen Presence and power of that which the renowned Tielhard de Chardin called "The Within".

I pray for the grace to wholeheartedly respond to that Echo within. Those things that I have sensed, recalled and identified with, connect with a still point and are accessed through this SIGN.

> What do I say to JESUS who speaks to me in this text?

Seven Signs

Reflection to listen.

I **listen** to 'felt' responses to the issues that this story encourages in me to effect **action**.

What is it that I yearn to move toward?

What does the Spirit of Jesus want me to do today?

Why did the 'Holy Spirit choose this **event** to effect an ACTION of Jesus?

I LISTEN to my heart, the core of my being, where the Holy Spirit moves and I speak to Jesus about any things that connect me with this Sign of Jesus.

I record the words, images or feelings that connect me with the compassionate feelings and actions of Jesus.

Words	*Feelings*	*Images*
↓	↓	↓

Seven Signs

Reflection for insight.

I have some insights regarding my own values and attitudes that compare with the attitudes of compassion, hospitality and inclusion of Jesus toward persons present in this event.

I have become aware that He has the desire and power to help me to improve or to develop my personal relationships with my family, my friends and with Him from the following:

A WORD from scripture	A value that Jesus exhibits
Some unique relationship that Jesus communicates.	Some personal enlightenment

Seven Signs

I reflect on the **values** that the characters portray for **insight** to clarify my own values.

Which characters?	What values do they exhibit?
_____	_____
_____	_____
_____	_____
_____	_____
_____	_____

I choose to 'step' into the persona or character of_____ with whom I empathise to become conscious that . . .

I too am called to:

- a new awareness
  e.g. _____
  _____

- a new
  perception _____
  _____

- a new enlightenment
  concerning _____
  _____

- a new application ie, action
  _____
  _____

Seven Signs

Some suggestions to **journal** my response to this Sign of Jesus.

Identification with the persona—

- I "become" one of the characters in this event and write "in role" from their perspective or perspectives.

I write—(of what happened in heart today when I met Jesus in this event).

- a letter to God, to Mary, or to my own inner spirit.
- a poem, prayer or lyric.
- about my reactions to any specific character.

I identify—

- the people I celebrate who are in my life.
- what I celebrate in my own life.
- my own differences.
- my own uniqueness.
- my own gifts, talents and capabilities.

I construct—

- what the symbols in this scene resemble or mean for me. (e.g. empty jars, wine, bread)
- a crossword puzzle with both questions and answers.

I draw—

- symbols that I've identified as having meaning that connect me with this Sign.

Seven Signs

Journal in response to the cure of the paralytic at the sheep pool   Date: / /

Seven Signs

Resolution

I ask for the grace to respond enthusiastically to the revelation I have received in this reflection on God's love, His intimacy and His power. I ask that God's name will be honoured and that God's reign will be achieved in me and in all people everywhere, as I make my resolutions.

	Long term goal	Short term goal	Daily goal
What is the goal?			
Why?			
Time frame of realising this goal			
I visualise myself achieving my goals and draw this.			

I make a personal affirmation _____

I isolate a mantra from the reading _____

Seven Signs

Cure of the Man at the Sheep Pool.
Mandala

I may have become aware of a central and powerful meaning from focusing on this event.

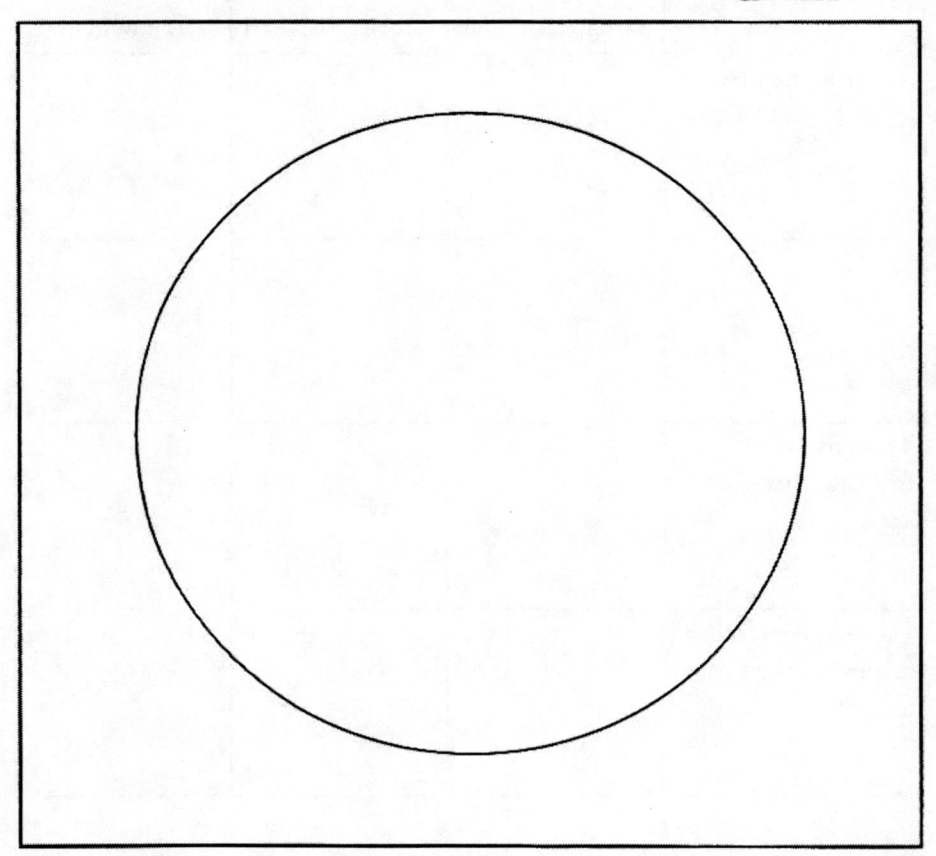

Perhaps to draw a meaningful symbol (that typifies, represents or recalls some idea or quality), within the mandala may register for me the power I've derived from considering or contemplating this sign.

Seven Signs

Recapitulation or Examine.

From reading about and contemplating the actions and attitudes of Jesus in this significant event, I have realised an aspect of the true nature and identity of Jesus-viz _____

This realisation has the power to call me to respond using the four functions of my psyche, to sense, to think, to feel emotionally and to use my intuition. It is this last function of intuition that *connects* me with the *risen presence of Jesus,* transferred to me in this event and that invites me to grow in love, patience, kindness and service toward my family and also within my social and professional world.

I visualise myself engaged in a particular situation where I am empowered to pray, to act with hospitality, compassion or patience in response to the persons whom I encounter in my life today. I draw this mental projection of myself acting positively, within the circular diagram.

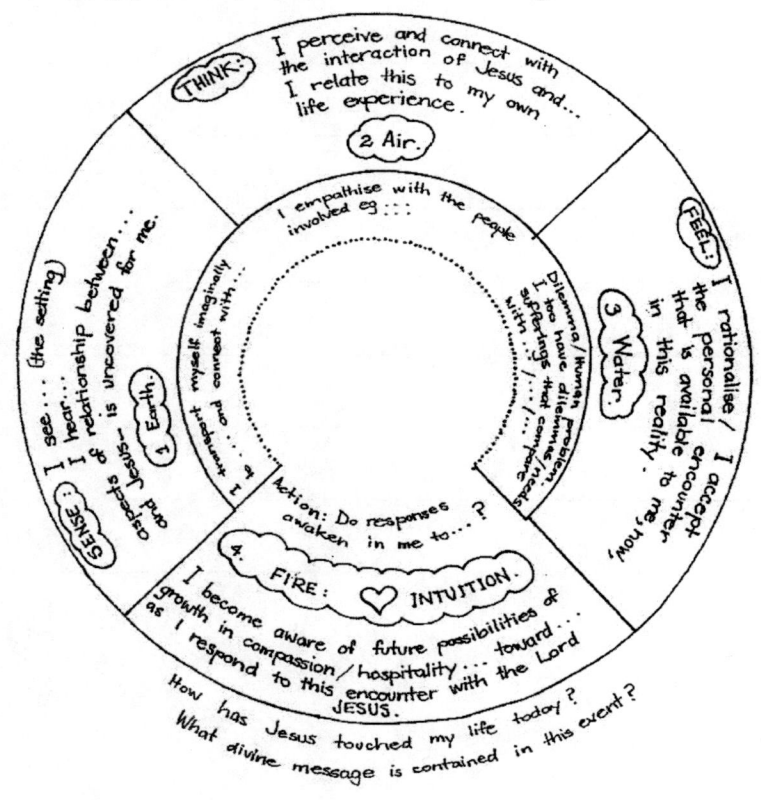

NOTES

NOTES

SEVEN SIGNS

MULTIPLICATION OF THE LOAVES

PART FOUR—FOURTH SIGN

Read—The multiplication of loaves Jn 6:1-15
Read—Outline the narrative
Read—Highlight any significant words or phrases
Read—Observe personal responses/relationships of characters

Reflect—Listen to your felt responses.
Reflect—Insights/values clarified.

Journal—Write "in role as any chosen character"
Resolution—Affirmation/prayer or mantra
Mandala—Draw essential idea.

Notes—Any connected personal ideas

Fourth Sign

**Multiplication of the Loaves.
Jn: 6: 1-15**

Reading to establish the literal meaning using the first level of imagery, the surface or sensory level.

¹ After this, Jesus went across the Sea of Galilee [of Tiberias]. ² A large crowd followed him, because they saw the signs he was performing on the sick. ³ Jesus went up on the mountain, and there he sat down with his disciples. ⁴ The Jewish feast of Passover was near. ⁵ When Jesus raised his eyes and saw that a large crowd was coming to him, he said to Philip, "Where can we buy enough food for them to eat?"⁶ He said this to test him, because he himself knew what he was going to do.⁷ Philip answered him, "Two hundred days' wages worth of food would not be enough for each of them to have a little [bit]. ⁸ One of his disciples, Andrew, the brother of Simon Peter, said to him, ⁹ "There is a boy here who has five barley loaves and two fish; but what good are these for so many?" ¹⁰ Jesus said, "Have the people recline." Now there was a great deal of grass in that place. So the men reclined, about five thousand in number. ¹¹ Then Jesus took the loaves, gave thanks, and distributed them to those who were reclining, and also as much of the fish as they wanted. ¹² When they had had their fill, he said to his disciples," Gather the fragments left over, so that nothing will be wasted."¹³ So they collected them, and filled twelve wicker baskets with fragments from the five barley loaves that had been more than they could eat.

¹⁴ When the people saw the sign he had done, they said "This is truly the Prophet, the one who is to come into the world." ¹⁵ Since Jesus knew that they were going to come and carry him off to make him king, he withdrew again to the mountain alone.

RESPONSE AT THE SENSORY LEVEL OF IMAGERY

Setting:.

- Where did the event take place?
- When (historically)?
- What was the event?

Characters;

- Who are the major characters?
- Who are the minor characters?

Dilemma or human problem;

- What was the problem?
- Who was affected by the problem?

Action.

- Who initiated a response?
- How did Jesus respond to this human problem?

Conclusion:

- What were the final results for the major characters?
- What were the results for minor characters?

What do I sense from this scene?

Fourth Sign

**Multiplication of the Loaves.
Jn: 6: 1-15**

Reading to establish the *second level of imagery,* the recollective/analytic level to evoke personal connected memories.

¹ After this, Jesus went across the Sea of Galilee [of Tiberias].² A large crowd followed him, because they saw the signs he was performing on the sick.³ Jesus went up on the mountain, and there he sat down with his disciples. ⁴ The Jewish feast of Passover was near. ⁵ When Jesus raised his eyes and saw that a large crowd was coming to him, he said to Philip, "Where can we buy enough food for them to eat?"⁶ He said this to test him, because he himself knew what he was going to do.⁷ Philip answered him, "Two hundred days' wages worth of food would not be enough for each of them to have a little [bit]. ⁸ One of his disciples, Andrew, the brother of Simon Peter, said to him, ⁹ "There is a boy here who has five barley loaves and two fish; but what good are these for so many?" ¹⁰ Jesus said, "Have the people recline." Now there was a great deal of grass in that place. So the men reclined, about five thousand in number. ¹¹ Then Jesus took the loaves, gave thanks, and distributed them to those who were reclining, and also as much of the fish as they wanted. ¹² When they had had their fill, he said to his disciples," Gather the fragments left over, so that nothing will be wasted."¹³ So they collected them, and filled twelve wicker baskets with fragments from the five barley loaves that had been more than they could eat.

¹⁴ When the people saw the sign he had done, they said "This is truly the Prophet, the one who is to come into the world." ¹⁵ Since Jesus knew that they were going to come and carry him off to make him king, he withdrew again to the mountain alone.

RESPONSE AT THE RECOLLECTIVE—ANALYTIC LEVEL OF IMAGERY.

Here I study my own past, my problems and my potentialities. Memories both verbal and visual are accessed as I analyse this narrative. I resonate parallels in my own life.

Narrative Structure: Diagram

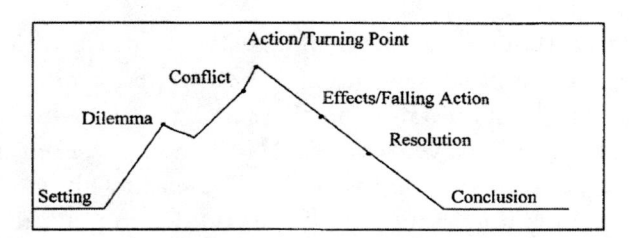

Setting:
- I transport myself imaginally to the place. _____
- I connect with a character of my choice viz _____

Characters—
- I empathise with a certain person viz _____
  or persons viz _____
  _____

The dilemma/human problem;
- I accept this as my own problem.
- I experience the suffering.
- I take on board the needs.

Action—
- I recognize my own potential to solve problems, to be proactive and to decide in favour of goal setting and positive intention to act.

Conclusion
- What are the final results for me from my identification with my chosen character?

What have I become more aware of?
- What message have I found in this scene that connects with memories in my own life experience?

Fourth Sign

Multiplication of the Loaves.
Jn: 6: 1-15

Reading to establish the *third level of imagery*, the symbolic level. This enables me to connect with mythical and archetypal figures. Here I find that symbols can have relevance to my life.

[1] After this, Jesus went across the Sea of Galilee [of Tiberias]. [2] A large crowd followed him, because they saw the signs he was performing on the sick. [3] Jesus went up on the mountain, and there he sat down with his disciples. [4] The Jewish feast of Passover was near. [5] When Jesus raised his eyes and saw that a large crowd was coming to him, he said to Philip, "Where can we buy enough food for them to eat?" [6] He said this to test him, because he himself knew what he was going to do. [7] Philip answered him, "Two hundred days' wages worth of food would not be enough for each of them to have a little [bit]. [8] One of his disciples, Andrew, the brother of Simon Peter, said to him, [9] "There is a boy here who has five barley loaves and two fish; but what good are these for so many?" [10] Jesus said, "Have the people recline." Now there was a great deal of grass in that place. So the men reclined, about five thousand in number. [11] Then Jesus took the loaves, gave thanks, and distributed them to those who were reclining, and also as much of the fish as they wanted. [12] When they had had their fill, he said to his disciples," Gather the fragments left over, so that nothing will be wasted."[13] So they collected them, and filled twelve wicker baskets with fragments from the five barley loaves that had been more than they could eat.

[14] When the people saw the sign he had done, they said "This is truly the Prophet, the one who is to come into the world." [15] Since Jesus knew that they were going to come and carry him off to make him king, he withdrew again to the mountain alone.

Seven Signs

RESPONSE AT THE SYMBOLIC LEVEL OF IMAGERY

I highlight words or phrases that symbolize and reflect patterns in my own personal life and its context. These symbolic images move me beyond my own personal-particular, toward more universal formulations. Here I'm able to experience a sense of continuity with evolutionary and historic process. I may identify with archetypical figures that have relevance to my own life and to my own problems.

Rational evaluation:

- I "become" this archetypal character to experience the facts of the situation, the values and relationship between this person and Jesus.
- I transfer this imaginal experience to my own real life situation.
- I observe the responsive action of Jesus toward _____
- I identify with the feelings of this character toward Jesus _____
- I observe the actions of other major characters _____
- I identify with the feelings of Jesus to this person _____
- I too participate in the feelings, needs and responses of the characters with whom I have chosen to identify.

The feelings and needs of the characters were connected, so that a final result occurred at that time and in that place.

From this consideration I choose a symbol that has power to recall for me the images that are now imprinted in my senses, in my memory and in my experience.

> I draw and label my chosen symbol.

The symbols I've selected have relevance to my own life as they represent my connection with my consciousness of sources of deep knowing and the reality of creative processes

Fourth Sign

Multiplication of the Loaves.
Jn: 6: 1-15

Reading to establish *the fourth level of imagery,* the integral level of my own experience. Here I find my own essence or "groundedness." I find a sense of new commitment to and communion with social, ecological and spiritual order. I gaze at the scene with love and become open to an awareness of order and presence.

[1] After this, Jesus went across the Sea of Galilee [of Tiberias].[2] A large crowd followed him, because they saw the signs he was performing on the sick.[3] Jesus went up on the mountain, and there he sat down with his disciples. [4] The Jewish feast of Passover was near. [5] When Jesus raised his eyes and saw that a large crowd was coming to him, he said to Philip, "Where can we buy enough food for them to eat?"[6] He said this to test him, because he himself knew what he was going to do.[7] Philip answered him, "Two hundred days' wages worth of food would not be enough for each of them to have a little [bit]. [8] One of his disciples, Andrew, the brother of Simon Peter, said to him, [9] "There is a boy here who has five barley loaves and two fish; but what good are these for so many?" [10] Jesus said, "Have the people recline." Now there was a great deal of grass in that place. So the men reclined, about five thousand in number. [11] Then Jesus took the loaves, gave thanks, and distributed them to those who were reclining, and also as much of the fish as they wanted. [12] When they had had their fill, he said to his disciples," Gather the fragments left over, so that nothing will be wasted."[13] So they collected them, and filled twelve wicker baskets with fragments from the five barley loaves that had been more than they could eat.

[14] When the people saw the sign he had done, they said "This is truly the Prophet, the one who is to come into the world." [15] Since Jesus knew that they were going to come and carry him off to make him king, he withdrew again to the mountain alone.

Seven Signs

RESPONSE AT THE INTEGRAL LEVEL OF IMAGERY

Herein I descend to a level of awareness in which I experience my own true essence or the 'Ground of my Being'. Here I'm enabled to find The Holy Grail', the Cornucopia, and to courageously "launch out into the deep". I experience that the universe outside, is reflected on the inside, and I find that Great Nature is contained within both. Images and archetypes can become for me structural forms that mirror to me, the wider reality of the energy of life. Persons portrayed in this human event experienced a new sightedness.

> In the light of the life, death and resurrection of Jesus, what does this text say to me?

I become aware of possibilities of involvement in deep contemplation, in works of compassion, of hospitality and generosity in response to the Risen Presence and power of that which the renowned Tielhard de Chardin called "The Within".

I pray for the grace to wholeheartedly respond to that Echo within. Those things that I have sensed, recalled and identified with, connect with a still point and are accessed through this SIGN.

> What do I say to JESUS who speaks to me in this text?

Seven Signs

Reflection to listen.

I listen to 'felt' responses to the issues that this story encourages in me to effect **action.**

What is it that I yearn to move toward?

What does the Spirit of Jesus want me to do today?

Why did the 'Holy Spirit choose this **event** to effect an ACTION of Jesus?

I LISTEN to my heart, the core of my being, where the Holy Spirit moves and I speak to Jesus about any things that connect me with this Sign of Jesus.

I record the words, images or feelings that connect me with the compassionate feelings and actions of Jesus.

Words	*Feelings*	*Images*
↓	↓	↓

Seven Signs

Reflection for insight.

I have some insights regarding my own values and attitudes that compare with the attitudes of compassion, hospitality and inclusion of Jesus toward persons present in this event.

I have become aware that He has the desire and power to help me to improve or to develop my personal relationships with my family, my friends and with Him from the following:

A WORD from scripture	A value that Jesus exhibits
Some unique relationship that Jesus communicates.	Some personal enlightenment

Seven Signs

I reflect on the **values** that the characters portray for **insight** to clarify my own values.

Which characters?	What values do they exhibit?
_____	_____
_____	_____
_____	_____
_____	_____

I choose to 'step' into the persona or character of _____
with whom I empathise to become conscious that . . .

I too am called to:

- a new awareness
  e.g. _____
  _____

- a new
  perception _____
  _____

- a new enlightenment
  concerning _____
  _____

- a new application ie, action
  _____
  _____

Seven Signs

Some suggestions to **journal** my response to this Sign of Jesus.

Identification with the persona—

- I "become" one of the characters in this event and write "in role" from their perspective or perspectives.

I write—(of what happened in heart today when I met Jesus in this event).

- a letter to God, to Mary, or to my own inner spirit.
- a poem, prayer or lyric.
- about my reactions to any specific character.

I identify—

- the people I celebrate who are in my life.
- what I celebrate in my own life.
- my own differences.
- my own uniqueness.
- my own gifts, talents and capabilities.

I construct—

- what the symbols in this scene resemble or mean for me. (e.g. empty jars, wine, bread)
- a crossword puzzle with both questions and answers.

I draw—

- symbols that I've identified as having meaning that connect me with this Sign.

Seven Signs

Journal in response to the multiplication of the loaves   Date: / / .

_____
_____
_____
_____
_____
_____
_____
_____
_____
_____
_____
_____
_____
_____
_____
_____

Seven Signs

Resolution

I ask for the grace to respond enthusiastically to the revelation I have received in this reflection on God's love, His intimacy and His power. I ask that God's name will be honoured and that God's reign will be achieved in me and in all people everywhere, as I make my resolutions.

	Long term goal	Short term goal	Daily goal
What is the goal?			
Why?			
Time frame of realising this goal			
I visualise myself achieving my goals and draw this.			

I make a personal affirmation _____

I isolate a mantra from the reading _____

Seven Signs

The Miracle of Loaves.
Mandala

I may have become aware of a central and powerful meaning from focusing on this event.

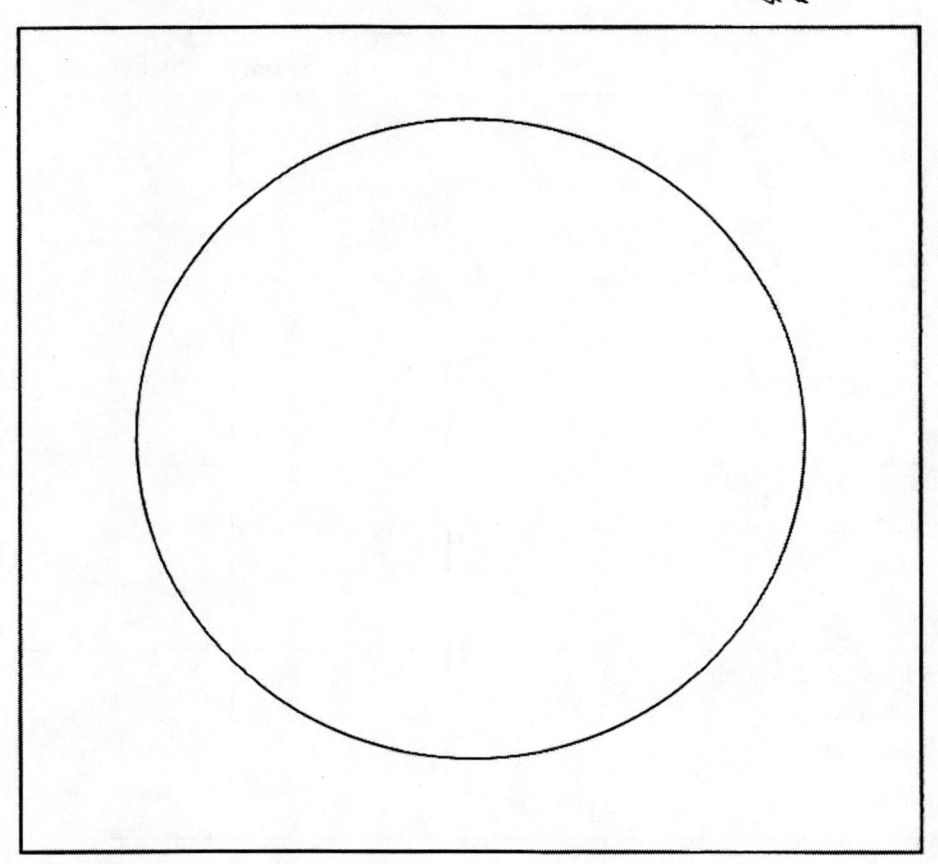

Perhaps to draw a meaningful symbol (that typifies, represents or recalls some idea or quality), within the mandala may register for me the power I've derived from considering or contemplating this sign.

SEVEN SIGNS OF ST. JOHN

Seven Signs

Recapitulation or Examine.

From reading about and contemplating the actions and attitudes of Jesus in this significant event, I have realised an aspect of the true nature and identity of Jesus-viz _____

This realisation has the power to call me to respond using the four functions of my psyche, to sense, to think, to feel emotionally and to use my intuition. It is this last function of intuition that *connects* me with the *risen presence of Jesus,* transferred to me in this event and that invites me to grow in love, patience, kindness and service toward my family and also within my social and professional world.

I visualise myself engaged in a particular situation where I am empowered to pray, to act with hospitality, compassion or patience in response to the persons whom I encounter in my life today. I draw this mental projection of myself acting positively, within the circular diagram.

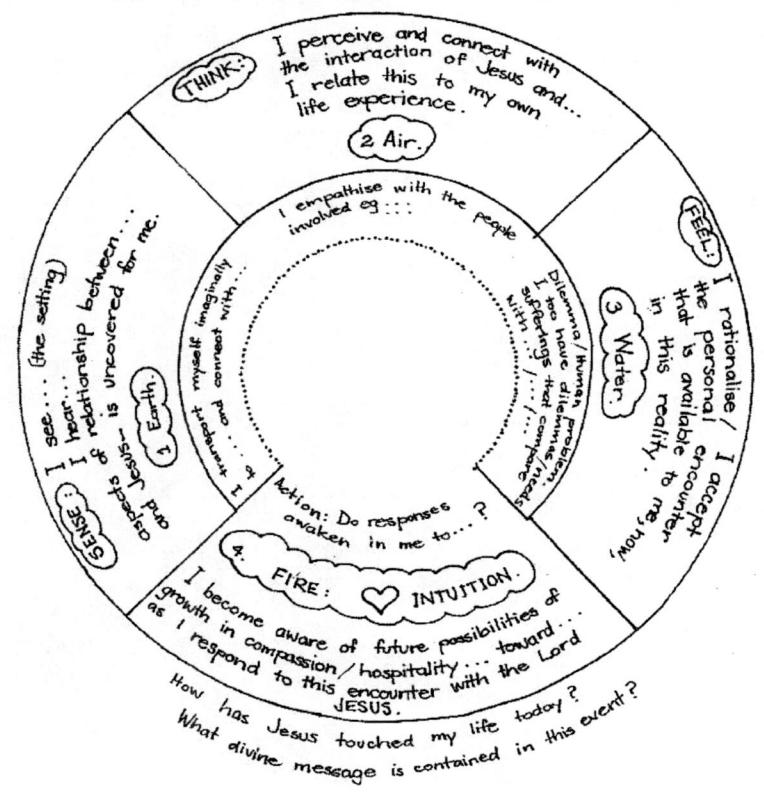

NOTES

NOTES

SEVEN SIGNS

JESUS WALKS ON THE SEA

JESUS REVEALS HIS NAME

PART FIVE—FIFTH SIGN

Read—Jesus walks on the sea Jn 6:16-21
Read—Outline the narrative
Read—Highlight any significant words or phrases
Read—Observe personal responses/relationships of characters

Reflect—Listen to your felt responses.
Reflect—Insights/values clarified.

Journal—Write "in role as any chosen character"
Resolution—Affirmation/prayer or mantra
Mandala—Draw essential idea.
Notes—Any connected personal ideas

Fifth Sign

Walking on the Water
Jn 6 : 16-21

Reading to establish the literal meaning using the first level of imagery, the surface or sensory level.

[16] When it was evening, his disciples went down to the sea, [17] embarked in a boat, and went across the sea to Capernaum. It had already grown dark, and Jesus had not yet come to them. [18] The sea was stirred up because a strong wind was blowing. [19] When they had rowed about three or four miles, they saw Jesus walking on the sea and coming near the boat, and they began to be afraid. [20] But he said to them, "It is I. Do not be afraid." [21] They wanted to take him into the boat, but the boat immediately arrived at the shore to which they were heading.

RESPONSE AT THE SENSORY LEVEL OF IMAGERY

Setting:.

- Where did the event take place?
- When (historically)?
- What was the event?

Characters;

- Who are the major characters?
- Who are the minor characters?

Dilemma or human problem;

- What was the problem?
- Who was affected by the problem?

Action.

- Who initiated a response?
- How did Jesus respond to this human problem?

Conclusion:

- What were the final results for the major characters?
- What were the results for minor characters?

What do I sense from this scene?

Fifth Sign

Walking on the Water
Jn 6 : 16-21

Reading to establish the *second level of imagery,* the recollective/analytic level to evoke personal connected memories.

[16] When it was evening, his disciples went down to the sea, [17] embarked in a boat, and went across the sea to Capernaum. It had already grown dark, and Jesus had not yet come to them. [18] The sea was stirred up because a strong wind was blowing. [19] When they had rowed about three or four miles, they saw Jesus walking on the sea and coming near the boat, and they began to be afraid. [20] But he said to them, "It is I. Do not be afraid." [21] They wanted to take him into the boat, but the boat immediately arrived at the shore to which they were heading.

RESPONSE AT THE RECOLLECTIVE—ANALYTIC LEVEL OF IMAGERY.

Here I study my own past, my problems and my potentialities. Memories both verbal and visual are accessed as I analyse this narrative. I resonate parallels in my own life.

Narrative Structure: Diagram

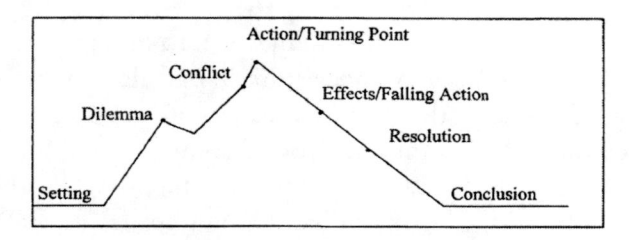

Setting:
- I transport myself imaginally to the place. _____
- I connect with a character of my choice viz _____

Characters—
- I empathise with a certain person viz _____
  or persons viz _____
  _____

The dilemma/human problem;
- I accept this as my own problem.
- I experience the suffering.
- I take on board the needs.

Action—
- I recognize my own potential to solve problems, to be proactive and to decide in favour of goal setting and positive intention to act.

Conclusion
- What are the final results for me from my identification with my chosen character?

What have I become more aware of?
- What message have I found in this scene that connects with memories in my own life experience?

Fifth Sign

Walking on the Water
Jn 6 : 16-21

Reading to establish the *third level of imagery*, the symbolic level. This enables me to connect with mythical and archetypal figures. Here I find that symbols can have relevance to my life.

[16] When it was evening, his disciples went down to the sea, [17] embarked in a boat, and went across the sea to Capernaum. It had already grown dark, and Jesus had not yet come to them. [18] The sea was stirred up because a strong wind was blowing. [19] When they had rowed about three or four miles, they saw Jesus walking on the sea and coming near the boat, and they began to be afraid. [20] But he said to them, "It is I. Do not be afraid." [21] They wanted to take him into the boat, but the boat immediately arrived at the shore to which they were heading.

Seven Signs

RESPONSE AT THE SYMBOLIC LEVEL OF IMAGERY

I highlight words or phrases that symbolize and reflect patterns in my own personal life and its context. These symbolic images move me beyond my own personal-particular, toward more universal formulations. Here I'm able to experience a sense of continuity with evolutionary and historic process. I may identify with archetypical figures that have relevance to my own life and to my own problems.

Rational evaluation:

- I "become" this archetypal character to experience the facts of the situation, the values and relationship between this person and Jesus.
- I transfer this imaginal experience to my own real life situation.
- I observe the responsive action of Jesus toward _____
- I identify with the feelings of this character toward Jesus _____
- I observe the actions of other major characters _____
- I identify with the feelings of Jesus to this person _____
- I too participate in the feelings, needs and responses of the characters with whom I have chosen to identify.

The feelings and needs of the characters were connected, so that a final result occurred at that time and in that place.

From this consideration I choose a symbol that has power to recall for me the images that are now imprinted in my senses, in my memory and in my experience.

> I draw and label my chosen symbol.

The symbols I've selected have relevance to my own life as they represent my connection with my consciousness of sources of deep knowing and the reality of creative processes

Fifth Sign

Walking on the Water
Jn 6 : 16-21

Reading to establish *the fourth level of imagery,* the integral level of my own experience. Here I find my own essence or "groundedness." I find a sense of new commitment to and communion with social, ecological and spiritual order. I gaze at the scene with love and become open to an awareness of order and presence.

[16] When it was evening, his disciples went down to the sea, [17] embarked in a boat, and went across the sea to Capernaum. It had already grown dark, and Jesus had not yet come to them. [18] The sea was stirred up because a strong wind was blowing. [19] When they had rowed about three or four miles, they saw Jesus walking on the sea and coming near the boat, and they began to be afraid. [20] But he said to them, "It is I. Do not be afraid." [21] They wanted to take him into the boat, but the boat immediately arrived at the shore to which they were heading.

Seven Signs

RESPONSE AT THE INTEGRAL LEVEL OF IMAGERY

Herein I descend to a level of awareness in which I experience my own true essence or the 'Ground of my Being'. Here I'm enabled to find The Holy Grail', the Cornucopia, and to courageously "launch out into the deep". I experience that the universe outside, is reflected on the inside, and I find that Great Nature is contained within both. Images and archetypes can become for me structural forms that mirror to me, the wider reality of the energy of life. Persons portrayed in this human event experienced a new sightedness.

> In the light of the life, death and resurrection of Jesus, what does this text say to me?

I become aware of possibilities of involvement in deep contemplation, in works of compassion, of hospitality and generosity in response to the Risen Presence and power of that which the renowned Tielhard de Chardin called "The Within".

I pray for the grace to wholeheartedly respond to that Echo within. Those things that I have sensed, recalled and identified with, connect with a still point and are accessed through this SIGN.

> What do I say to JESUS who speaks to me in this text?

Seven Signs

Reflection to listen.

I listen to 'felt' responses to the issues that this story encourages in me to effect **action**.

What is it that I yearn to move toward?

What does the Spirit of Jesus want me to do today?

Why did the 'Holy Spirit choose this **event** to effect an ACTION of Jesus?

I LISTEN to my heart, the core of my being, where the Holy Spirit moves and I speak to Jesus about any things that connect me with this Sign of Jesus.

I record the words, images or feelings that connect me with the compassionate feelings and actions of Jesus.

Words	*Feelings*	*Images*
↓	↓	↓

Seven Signs

Reflection for insight.

I have some insights regarding my own values and attitudes that compare with the attitudes of compassion, hospitality and inclusion of Jesus toward persons present in this event.

I have become aware that He has the desire and power to help me to improve or to develop my personal relationships with my family, my friends and with Him from the following:

A WORD from scripture	A value that Jesus exhibits
Some unique relationship that Jesus communicates.	Some personal enlightenment

Seven Signs

I reflect on the **values** that the characters portray for **insight** to clarify my own values.

Which characters?	What values do they exhibit?
_____	_____
_____	_____
_____	_____
_____	_____
_____	_____

I choose to 'step' into the persona or character of_____
with whom I empathise to become conscious that . . .

I too am called to:

- a new awareness
  e.g. _____
  _____

- a new
  perception _____
  _____

- a new enlightenment
  concerning _____
  _____

- a new application ie, action
  _____
  _____

Seven Signs

Some suggestions to **journal** my response to this Sign of Jesus.

Identification with the persona—

- I "become" one of the characters in this event and write "in role" from their perspective or perspectives.

I write—(of what happened in heart today when I met Jesus in this event).

- a letter to God, to Mary, or to my own inner spirit.
- a poem, prayer or lyric.
- about my reactions to any specific character.

I identify—

- the people I celebrate who are in my life.
- what I celebrate in my own life.
- my own differences.
- my own uniqueness.
- my own gifts, talents and capabilities.

I construct—

- what the symbols in this scene resemble or mean for me. (e.g. empty jars, wine, bread)
- a crossword puzzle with both questions and answers.

I draw—

- symbols that I've identified as having meaning that connect me with this Sign.

Seven Signs

Journal in response to Jesus who walked on the sea.　　　　Date: / / .

___
___
___
___
___
___
___
___
___
___
___
___
___
___
___

Seven Signs

Resolution

I ask for the grace to respond enthusiastically to the revelation I have received in this reflection on God's love, His intimacy and His power. I ask that God's name will be honoured and that God's reign will be achieved in me and in all people everywhere, as I make my resolutions.

	Long term goal	Short term goal	Daily goal
What is the goal?			
Why?			
Time frame of realising this goal			
I visualise myself achieving my goals and draw this.			

I make a personal affirmation _____

I isolate a mantra from the reading _____

Seven Signs

Jesus Walks on the Sea.
Mandala

I may have become aware of a central and powerful meaning from focusing on this event.

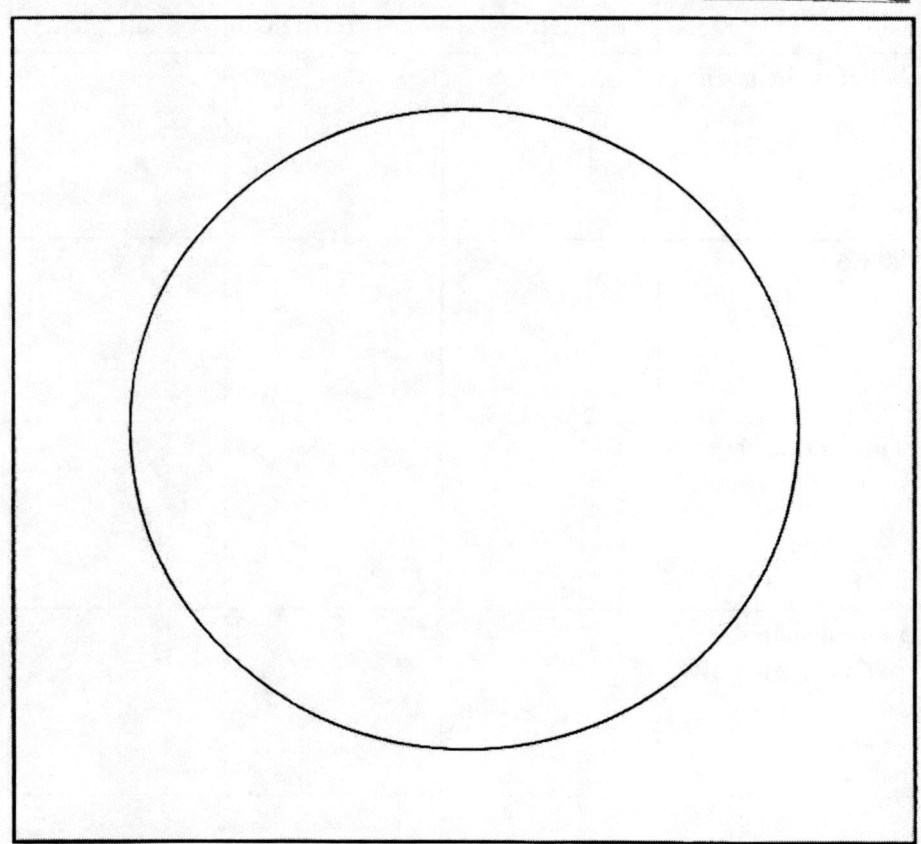

Perhaps to draw a meaningful symbol (that typifies, represents or recalls some idea or quality), within the mandala may register for me the power I've derived from considering or contemplating this sign.

SEVEN SIGNS OF ST. JOHN

Seven Signs

Recapitulation or Examine.

From reading about and contemplating the actions and attitudes of Jesus in this significant event, I have realised an aspect of the true nature and identity of Jesus-viz ——————————

This realisation has the power to call me to respond using the four functions of my psyche, to sense, to think, to feel emotionally and to use my intuition. It is this last function of intuition that *connects* me with the *risen presence of Jesus,* transferred to me in this event and that invites me to grow in love, patience, kindness and service toward my family and also within my social and professional world.

I visualise myself engaged in a particular situation where I am empowered to pray, to act with hospitality, compassion or patience in response to the persons whom I encounter in my life today. I draw this mental projection of myself acting positively, within the circular diagram.

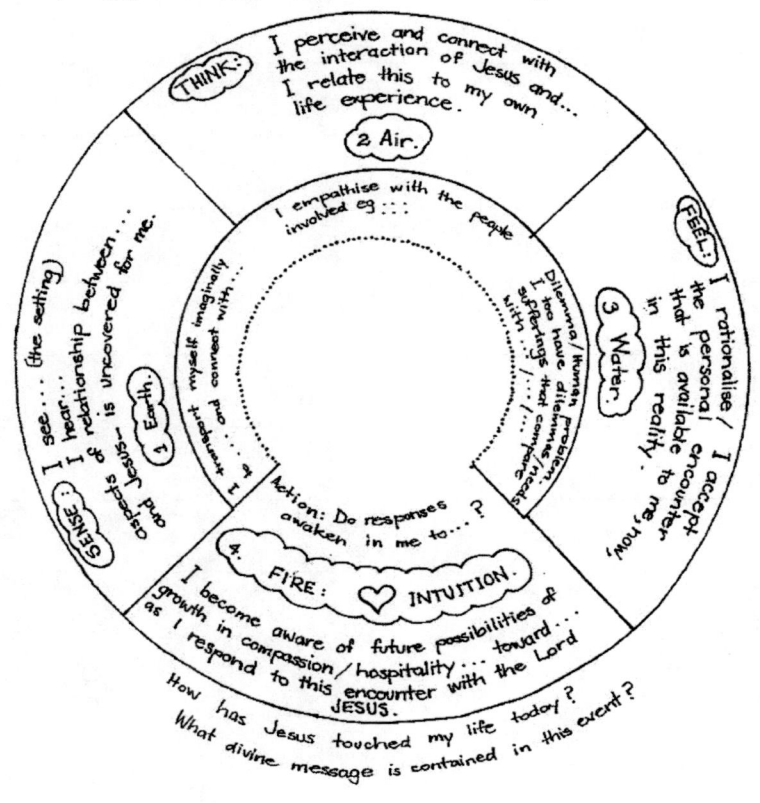

THINK: I perceive and connect with the interaction of Jesus and... I relate this to my own life experience.

2. Air.

I empathise with the people involved eg :::

FEEL: I rationalise / I accept the personal encounter that is available to me in this reality now.

3. Water. Dilemma / Human problems / too have dilemmas / sufferings that compare...

SENSE: I see... I hear... (the setting) aspects of relationship between... Jesus-is uncovered for me.

1. Earth.

I project myself imaginatively and connect with...

Action: Do responses awaken in me to...?

4. FIRE: ♡ INTUITION.

I become aware of future possibilities of growth in compassion / hospitality... toward as I respond to this encounter with the Lord JESUS.

How has Jesus touched my life today? What divine message is contained in this event?

NOTES

NOTES

SEVEN SIGNS

JESUS CURED A MAN WHO WAS BLIND FROM BIRTH

JESUS REVEALS HIS IDENTITY

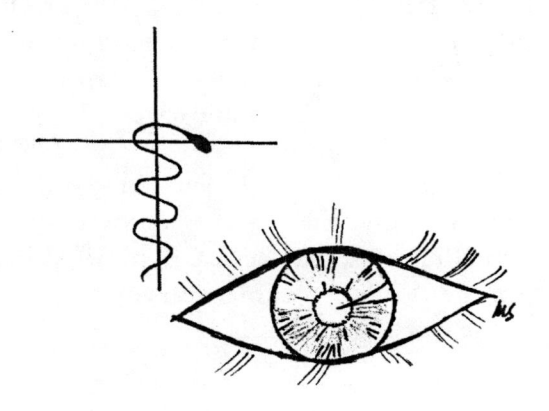

PART SIX—SIXTH SIGN

Read—Jesus cures a man who was blind from birth. Jn 9:1-9
Read—Outline the narrative
Read—Highlight any significant words or phrases
Read—Observe personal responses/relationships of characters

Reflect—Listen to your felt responses.
Reflect—Insights/values clarified.

Journal—Write "in role as any chosen character"
Resolution—Affirmation/prayer or mantra
Mandala—Draw essential idea.
Notes—Any connected personal ideas

Sixth Sign

Jesus cures a man who was blind from birth.
Jn 9:1-9 /35-38

Reading to establish the literal meaning using the first level of imagery, the surface or sensory level.

¹ As he passed by, he saw a man blind from birth. ² His disciples asked him, "Rabbi, who sinned this man or his parents, that he was born blind?"³ Jesus answered, "Neither he nor his parents sinned; it is so that the works of God might be made visible through him.⁴ We have to do the works of the one who sent me while it is day. Night is coming when no one can work. ⁵ While I am in the world, I am the light of the world."⁶ When he had said this, he spat on the ground and made clay with saliva, and smeared the clay on his eyes,⁷ and said to him "Go wash in the Pool of Siloam."(which means Sent). So he went and washed and came back able to see.

. . . ³⁵ When Jesus heard that they had thrown him out [of the Temple], he found him and said, "Do you believe in the Son of Man?" ³⁶ He answered and said, "Who is he, sir, that I may believe in him?" ³⁷ Jesus said to him, "You have seen him and the one speaking with you is he." ³⁸ He said, "I do believe, Lord," and he worshipped him.

RESPONSE AT THE SENSORY LEVEL OF IMAGERY

Setting:.

- Where did the event take place?
- When (historically)?
- What was the event?

Characters;

- Who are the major characters?
- Who are the minor characters?

Dilemma or human problem;

- What was the problem?
- Who was affected by the problem?

Action.

- Who initiated a response?
- How did Jesus respond to this human problem?

Conclusion:

- What were the final results for the major characters?
- What were the results for minor characters?

What do I sense from this scene?

Sixth Sign

**Jesus cures a man who was blind from birth.
Jn 9:1-9 /35-38**

Reading to establish the *second level of imagery,* the recollective/analytic level to evoke personal connected memories.

¹ As he passed by, he saw a man blind from birth. ² His disciples asked him, "Rabbi, who sinned this man or his parents, that he was born blind?" ³ Jesus answered, "Neither he nor his parents sinned; it is so that the works of God might be made visible through him. ⁴ We have to do the works of the one who sent me while it is day. Night is coming when no one can work. ⁵ While I am in the world, I am the light of the world." ⁶ When he had said this, he spat on the ground and made clay with saliva, and smeared the clay on his eyes,⁷ and said to him "Go wash in the Pool of Siloam."(which means Sent). So he went and washed and came back able to see.

. . . ³⁵ When Jesus heard that they had thrown him out [of the Temple], he found him and said, "Do you believe in the Son of Man?" ³⁶ He answered and said, "Who is he, sir, that I may believe in him?" ³⁷ Jesus said to him, "You have seen him and the one speaking with you is he." ³⁸ He said, "I do believe, Lord," and he worshipped him.

RESPONSE AT THE RECOLLECTIVE—ANALYTIC LEVEL OF IMAGERY.

Here I study my own past, my problems and my potentialities. Memories both verbal and visual are accessed as I analyse this narrative. I resonate parallels in my own life.

Narrative Structure: Diagram

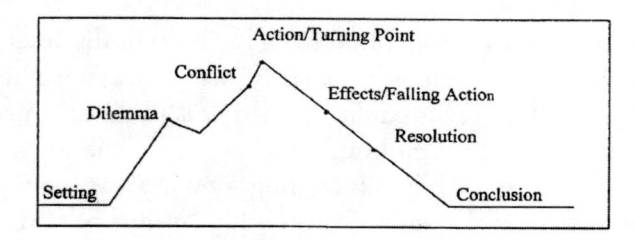

```
                    Action/Turning Point
           Conflict
                    Effects/Falling Action
    Dilemma
                        Resolution
Setting                         Conclusion
```

Setting:
- I transport myself imaginally to the place. _____
- I connect with a character of my choice viz _____

Characters—
- I empathise with a certain person viz _____
  or persons viz _____
  _____

The dilemma/human problem;
- I accept this as my own problem.
- I experience the suffering.
- I take on board the needs.

Action—
- I recognize my own potential to solve problems, to be proactive and to decide in favour of goal setting and positive intention to act.

Conclusion
- What are the final results for me from my identification with my chosen character?

What have I become more aware of?
- What message have I found in this scene that connects with memories in my own life experience?

Sixth Sign

Jesus cures a man who was blind from birth.
Jn 9:1-9 /35-38

Reading to establish the *third level of imagery*, the symbolic level. This enables me to connect with mythical and archetypal figures. Here I find that symbols can have relevance to my life.

[1] As he passed by, he saw a man blind from birth. [2] His disciples asked him, "Rabbi, who sinned this man or his parents, that he was born blind?" [3] Jesus answered, "Neither he nor his parents sinned; it is so that the works of God might be made visible through him. [4] We have to do the works of the one who sent me while it is day. Night is coming when no one can work. [5] While I am in the world, I am the light of the world." [6] When he had said this, he spat on the ground and made clay with saliva, and smeared the clay on his eyes, [7] and said to him "Go wash in the Pool of Siloam."(which means Sent). So he went and washed and came back able to see.

... [35] When Jesus heard that they had thrown him out [of the Temple], he found him and said, "Do you believe in the Son of Man?" [36] He answered and said, "Who is he, sir, that I may believe in him?" [37] Jesus said to him, "You have seen him and the one speaking with you is he." [38] He said, "I do believe, Lord," and he worshipped him.

Seven Signs

RESPONSE AT THE SYMBOLIC LEVEL OF IMAGERY

I highlight words or phrases that symbolize and reflect patterns in my own personal life and its context. These symbolic images move me beyond my own personal-particular, toward more universal formulations. Here I'm able to experience a sense of continuity with evolutionary and historic process. I may identify with archetypical figures that have relevance to my own life and to my own problems.

Rational evaluation:

- I "become" this archetypal character to experience the facts of the situation, the values and relationship between this person and Jesus.
- I transfer this imaginal experience to my own real life situation.
- I observe the responsive action of Jesus toward _____
- I identify with the feelings of this character toward Jesus _____
- I observe the actions of other major characters _____
- I identify with the feelings of Jesus to this person _____
- I too participate in the feelings, needs and responses of the characters with whom I have chosen to identify.

The feelings and needs of the characters were connected, so that a final result occurred at that time and in that place.

From this consideration I choose a symbol that has power to recall for me the images that are now imprinted in my senses, in my memory and in my experience.

I draw and label my chosen symbol.

The symbols I've selected have relevance to my own life as they represent my connection with my consciousness of sources of deep knowing and the reality of creative processes

Sixth Sign

Jesus cures a man who was blind from birth.
Jn 9:1-9 /35-38

Reading to establish *the fourth level of imagery,* the integral level of my own experience. Here I find my own essence or "groundedness." I find a sense of new commitment to and communion with social, ecological and spiritual order. I gaze at the scene with love and become open to an awareness of order and presence.

¹ As he passed by, he saw a man blind from birth. ² His disciples asked him, "Rabbi, who sinned this man or his parents, that he was born blind?"³ Jesus answered, "Neither he nor his parents sinned; it is so that the works of God might be made visible through him.⁴ We have to do the works of the one who sent me while it is day. Night is coming when no one can work. ⁵ While I am in the world, I am the light of the world."⁶ When he had said this, he spat on the ground and made clay with saliva, and smeared the clay on his eyes,⁷ and said to him "Go wash in the Pool of Siloam."(which means Sent). So he went and washed and came back able to see.

. . . ³⁵ When Jesus heard that they had thrown him out [of the Temple], he found him and said, "Do you believe in the Son of Man?" ³⁶ He answered and said, "Who is he, sir, that I may believe in him?" ³⁷ Jesus said to him, "You have seen him and the one speaking with you is he." ³⁸ He said, "I do believe, Lord," and he worshipped him.

Seven Signs

RESPONSE AT THE INTEGRAL LEVEL OF IMAGERY

Herein I descend to a level of awareness in which I experience my own true essence or the 'Ground of my Being'. Here I'm enabled to find The Holy Grail', the Cornucopia, and to courageously "launch out into the deep". I experience that the universe outside, is reflected on the inside, and I find that Great Nature is contained within both. Images and archetypes can become for me structural forms that mirror to me, the wider reality of the energy of life. Persons portrayed in this human event experienced a new sightedness.

> In the light of the life, death and resurrection of Jesus, what does this text say to me?

I become aware of possibilities of involvement in deep contemplation, in works of compassion, of hospitality and generosity in response to the Risen Presence and power of that which the renowned Tielhard de Chardin called "The Within".

I pray for the grace to wholeheartedly respond to that Echo within. Those things that I have sensed, recalled and identified with, connect with a still point and are accessed through this SIGN.

> What do I say to JESUS who speaks to me in this text?

Seven Signs

Reflection to listen.

I listen to 'felt' responses to the issues that this story encourages in me to effect **action.**

What is it that I yearn to move toward?

What does the Spirit of Jesus want me to do today?

Why did the 'Holy Spirit choose this **event** to effect an ACTION of Jesus?

I LISTEN to my heart, the core of my being, where the Holy Spirit moves and I speak to Jesus about any things that connect me with this Sign of Jesus.

I record the words, images or feelings that connect me with the compassionate feelings and actions of Jesus.

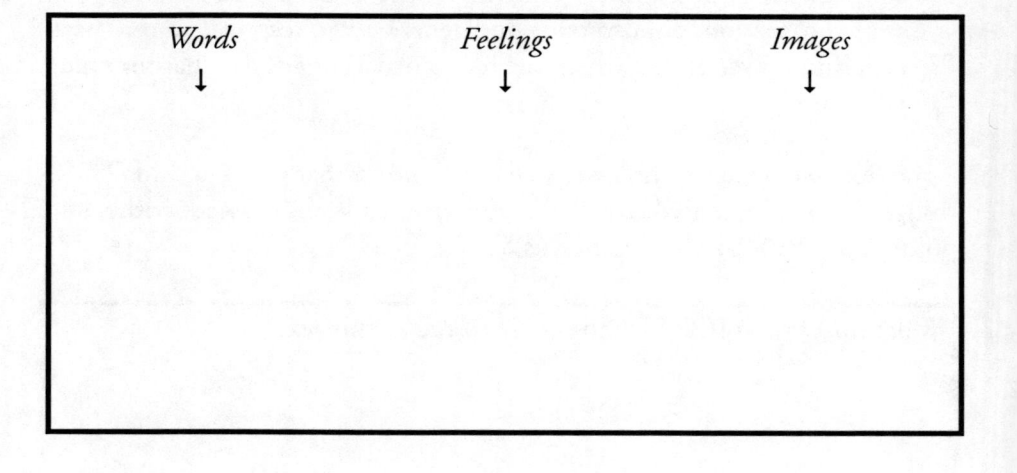

Words ↓	*Feelings* ↓	*Images* ↓

Seven Signs

Reflection for insight.

I have some insights regarding my own values and attitudes that compare with the attitudes of compassion, hospitality and inclusion of Jesus toward persons present in this event.

I have become aware that He has the desire and power to help me to improve or to develop my personal relationships with my family, my friends and with Him from the following:

A WORD from scripture	A value that Jesus exhibits
Some unique relationship that Jesus communicates.	Some personal enlightenment

Seven Signs

I reflect on the **values** that the characters portray for **insight** to clarify my own values.

Which characters?	What values do they exhibit?
_____	_____
_____	_____
_____	_____
_____	_____

I choose to 'step' into the persona or character of _____
with whom I empathise to become conscious that . . .

I too am called to:

- a new awareness
  e.g. _____
  _____

- a new
  perception _____

- a new enlightenment
  concerning _____
  _____

- a new application ie, action
  _____

Seven Signs

Some suggestions to **journal** my response to this Sign of Jesus.

Identification with the persona—

- I "become" one of the characters in this event and write "in role" from their perspective or perspectives.

I write—(of what happened in heart today when I met Jesus in this event).

- a letter to God, to Mary, or to my own inner spirit.
- a poem, prayer or lyric.
- about my reactions to any specific character.

I identify—

- the people I celebrate who are in my life.
- what I celebrate in my own life.
- my own differences.
- my own uniqueness.
- my own gifts, talents and capabilities.

I construct—

- what the symbols in this scene resemble or mean for me. (e.g. empty jars, wine, bread)
- a crossword puzzle with both questions and answers.

I draw—

- symbols that I've identified as having meaning that connect me with this Sign.

Seven Signs

Journal in response to the cure of the man who was blind from birth.   Date: / / .

Seven Signs

Resolution

I ask for the grace to respond enthusiastically to the revelation I have received in this reflection on God's love, His intimacy and His power. I ask that God's name will be honoured and that God's reign will be achieved in me and in all people everywhere, as **I** make my resolutions.

	Long term goal	Short term goal	Daily goal
What is the goal?			
Why?			
Time frame of realising this goal			
I visualise myself achieving my goals and draw this.			

I make a personal affirmation _____

I isolate a mantra from the reading _____

Seven Signs

Jesus Cures the Blind Man.
Mandala

I may have become aware of a central and powerful meaning from focusing on this event.

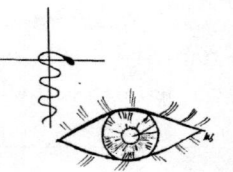

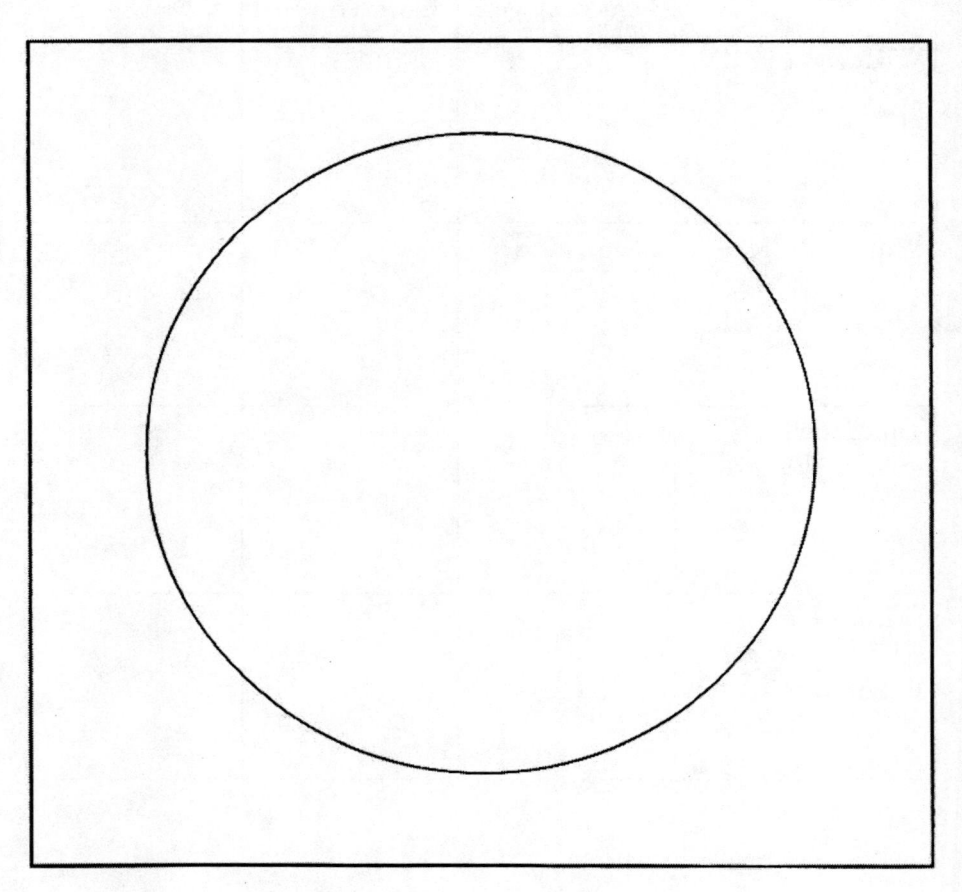

Perhaps to draw a meaningful symbol (that typifies, represents or recalls some idea or quality), within the mandala may register for me the power I've derived from considering or contemplating this sign.

SEVEN SIGNS OF ST. JOHN

Seven Signs

Recapitulation or Examine.

From reading about and contemplating the actions and attitudes of Jesus in this significant event, I have realised an aspect of the true nature and identity of Jesus-viz _____

This realisation has the power to call me to respond using the four functions of my psyche, to sense, to think, to feel emotionally and to use my intuition. It is this last function of intuition that *connects* me with the *risen presence of Jesus,* transferred to me in this event and that invites me to grow in love, patience, kindness and service toward my family and also within my social and professional world.

I visualise myself engaged in a particular situation where I am empowered to pray, to act with hospitality, compassion or patience in response to the persons whom I encounter in my life today. I draw this mental projection of myself acting positively, within the circular diagram.

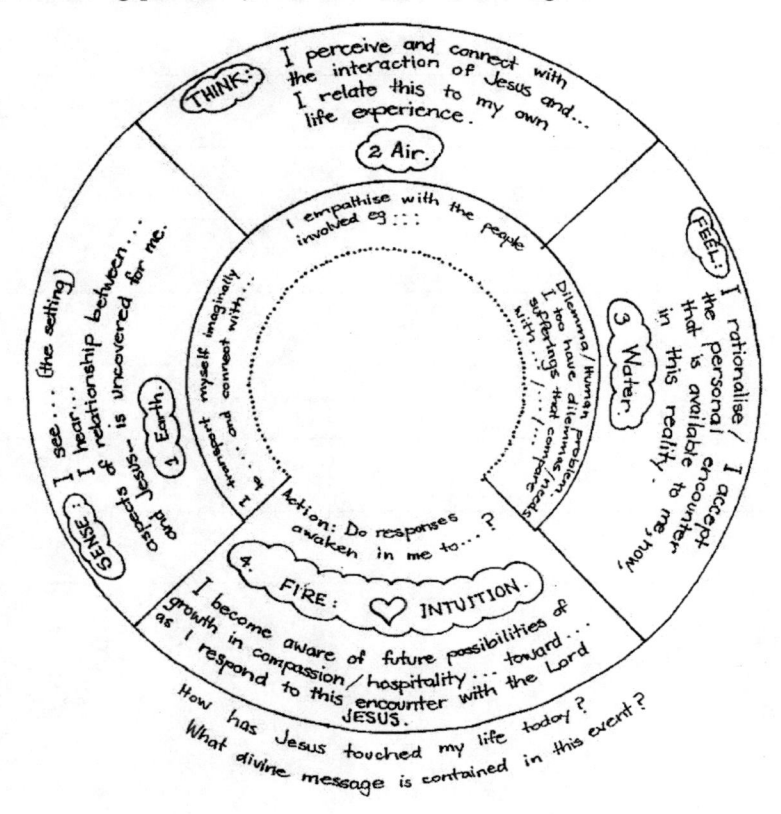

THINK: I perceive and connect with the interaction of Jesus and... I relate this to my own life experience.

2. Air

I empathise with the people involved eg :::

SENSE: I see... (the setting) I hear... aspects of relationship between... Jesus is uncovered for me.

1. Earth

I present myself imaginatively and connect with...

Dilemma / Human problem / sufferings that confronts / too have dilemmas in this reality.

3. Water

FEEL: I rationalise / I accept the personal encounter that is available to me now.

Action: Do responses awaken in me to...?

4. FIRE: ♡ INTUITION.

I become aware of future possibilities of growth in compassion / hospitality... toward... as I respond to this encounter with the Lord JESUS.

How has Jesus touched my life today? What divine message is contained in this event?

NOTES

NOTES

SEVEN SIGNS

JESUS RAISES LAZARUS FROM THE DEAD

PART SEVEN (a)—SEVENTH SIGN

Read—Jesus called forth Lazarus from death. Jn 11:1-20
Read—Outline the narrative
Read—Highlight any significant words or phrases
Read—Observe personal responses/relationships of characters

Reflect—Listen to your felt responses.
Reflect—Insights/values clarified.

Journal—Write "in role as any chosen character"
Resolution—Affirmation/prayer or mantra
Mandala—Draw essential idea.
Notes—Any connected personal ideas

Seventh Sign

Jesus raises Lazarus from the dead
Jn. 11:1-20

Reading to establish the literal meaning using the first level of imagery, the surface or sensory level.

[1.] Now a man was ill, Lazarus from Bethany, the village of Mary and her sister Martha. [2] Mary was the one who had anointed the Lord with perfumed oil and dried his feet with her hair; it was her brother Lazarus who was ill. [3] So the sisters sent word to him, saying, "Master, the one you love is ill." [4] When Jesus heard this he said, "This illness is not to end in death, but is for the glory of God, that the Son of God may be glorified through it."[5] Now Jesus loved Martha and her sister and Lazarus. [6] So that when he heard that he was ill, he remained for two days in the place where he was. [7] Then after this he said to his disciples "Let us go back to Judea." [8] The disciples said to him, "Rabbi, the Jews were just trying to stone you, and you want to go back there?" [9] Jesus answered, "Are there not twelve hours in a day? If one walks during the day, he does not stumble, because he sees the light of this world.[10] But if one walks at night, he stumbles, because the light is not in him." [11] He said this, and then told them," Our friend Lazarus is asleep, but I am going to awaken him." [12] So the disciples said to him, "Master, if he is asleep he will be saved." [13] But Jesus was talking about his death, while they thought that he meant ordinary sleep. [14] So then Jesus said to them clearly, "Lazarus has died. [15] And I am glad for you that I was not there, that you may believe. Let us go to him." [16] So Thomas called Didymus, said to his fellow disciples "Let us also go to die with him." [17] When Jesus arrived, he found that Lazarus had already been in the tomb for four days. [18] Now Bethany was near Jerusalem, only about two miles away. [19] And many of the Jews had come to Martha and Mary to comfort them about their brother. [20] When Martha heard that Jesus was coming, she went to meet him, but Mary sat at home.

RESPONSE AT THE SENSORY LEVEL OF IMAGERY

Setting:.

- Where did the event take place?
- When (historically)?
- What was the event?

Characters;

- Who are the major characters?
- Who are the minor characters?

Dilemma or human problem;

- What was the problem?
- Who was affected by the problem?

Action.

- Who initiated a response?
- How did Jesus respond to this human problem?

Conclusion:

- What were the final results for the major characters?
- What were the results for minor characters?

What do I sense from this scene?

Seventh Sign

Jesus raises Lazarus from the dead
Jn. 11:1-20

Reading to establish the *second level of imagery*, the recollective/analytic level to evoke personal connected memories.

[1.] Now a man was ill, Lazarus from Bethany, the village of Mary and her sister Martha. [2] Mary was the one who had anointed the Lord with perfumed oil and dried his feet with her hair; it was her brother Lazarus who was ill. [3] So the sisters sent word to him, saying, "Master, the one you love is ill." [4] When Jesus heard this he said, "This illness is not to end in death, but is for the glory of God, that the Son of God may be glorified through it."[5] Now Jesus loved Martha and her sister and Lazarus. [6] So that when he heard that he was ill, he remained for two days in the place where he was. [7] Then after this he said to his disciples "Let us go back to Judea." [8] The disciples said to him, "Rabbi, the Jews were just trying to stone you, and you want to go back there?" [9] Jesus answered, "Are there not twelve hours in a day? If one walks during the day, he does not stumble, because he sees the light of this world.[10] But if one walks at night, he stumbles, because the light is not in him." [11] He said this, and then told them," Our friend Lazarus is asleep, but I am going to awaken him." [12] So the disciples said to him, "Master, if he is asleep he will be saved." [13] But Jesus was talking about his death, while they thought that he meant ordinary sleep. [14] So then Jesus said to them clearly, "Lazarus has died. [15] And I am glad for you that I was not there, that you may believe. Let us go to him." [16] So Thomas called Didymus, said to his fellow disciples "Let us also go to die with him." [17] When Jesus arrived, he found that Lazarus had already been in the tomb for four days. [18] Now Bethany was near Jerusalem, only about two miles away. [19] And many of the Jews had come to Martha and Mary to comfort them about their brother. [20] When Martha heard that Jesus was coming, she went to meet him, but Mary sat at home.

RESPONSE AT THE RECOLLECTIVE—ANALYTIC LEVEL OF IMAGERY.

Here I study my own past, my problems and my potentialities. Memories both verbal and visual are accessed as I analyse this narrative. I resonate parallels in my own life.

Narrative Structure: Diagram

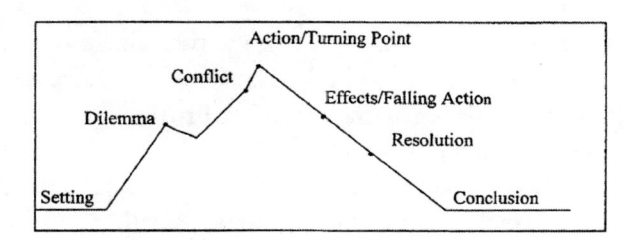

```
                    Action/Turning Point
            Conflict
                        Effects/Falling Action
      Dilemma
                          Resolution
Setting                         Conclusion
```

Setting:
- I transport myself imaginally to the place. _____
- I connect with a character of my choice viz _____

Characters—
- I empathise with a certain person viz _____
  or persons viz _____
  _____

The dilemma/human problem;
- I accept this as my own problem.
- I experience the suffering.
- I take on board the needs.

Action—
- I recognize my own potential to solve problems, to be proactive and to decide in favour of goal setting and positive intention to act.

Conclusion
- What are the final results for me from my identification with my chosen character?

What have I become more aware of?
- What message have I found in this scene that connects with memories in my own life experience?

Seventh Sign

Jesus raises Lazarus from the dead
Jn. 11:1-20

Reading to establish the *third level of imagery*, the symbolic level. This enables me to connect with mythical and archetypal figures. Here I find that symbols can have relevance to my life.

[1.] Now a man was ill, Lazarus from Bethany, the village of Mary and her sister Martha. [2] Mary was the one who had anointed the Lord with perfumed oil and dried his feet with her hair; it was her brother Lazarus who was ill. [3] So the sisters sent word to him, saying, "Master, the one you love is ill." [4] When Jesus heard this he said, "This illness is not to end in death, but is for the glory of God, that the Son of God may be glorified through it."[5] Now Jesus loved Martha and her sister and Lazarus. [6] So that when he heard that he was ill, he remained for two days in the place where he was. [7] Then after this he said to his disciples "Let us go back to Judea." [8] The disciples said to him, "Rabbi, the Jews were just trying to stone you, and you want to go back there?" [9] Jesus answered, "Are there not twelve hours in a day? If one walks during the day, he does not stumble, because he sees the light of this world.[10] But if one walks at night, he stumbles, because the light is not in him." [11] He said this, and then told them," Our friend Lazarus is asleep, but I am going to awaken him." [12] So the disciples said to him, "Master, if he is asleep he will be saved." [13] But Jesus was talking about his death, while they thought that he meant ordinary sleep. [14] So then Jesus said to them clearly, "Lazarus has died. [15] And I am glad for you that I was not there, that you may believe. Let us go to him." [16] So Thomas called Didymus, said to his fellow disciples "Let us also go to die with him." [17] When Jesus arrived, he found that Lazarus had already been in the tomb for four days. [18] Now Bethany was near Jerusalem, only about two miles away. [19] And many of the Jews had come to Martha and Mary to comfort them about their brother. [20] When Martha heard that Jesus was coming, she went to meet him, but Mary sat at home.

Seven Signs

RESPONSE AT THE SYMBOLIC LEVEL OF IMAGERY

I highlight words or phrases that symbolize and reflect patterns in my own personal life and its context. These symbolic images move me beyond my own personal-particular, toward more universal formulations. Here I'm able to experience a sense of continuity with evolutionary and historic process. I may identify with archetypical figures that have relevance to my own life and to my own problems.

Rational evaluation:

- I "become" this archetypal character to experience the facts of the situation, the values and relationship between this person and Jesus.
- I transfer this imaginal experience to my own real life situation.
- I observe the responsive action of Jesus toward _____
- I identify with the feelings of this character toward Jesus _____
- I observe the actions of other major characters _____
- I identify with the feelings of Jesus to this person _____
- I too participate in the feelings, needs and responses of the characters with whom I have chosen to identify.

The feelings and needs of the characters were connected, so that a final result occurred at that time and in that place.

From this consideration I choose a symbol that has power to recall for me the images that are now imprinted in my senses, in my memory and in my experience.

> I draw and label my chosen symbol.

The symbols I've selected have relevance to my own life as they represent my connection with my consciousness of sources of deep knowing and the reality of creative processes

Seventh Sign

Jesus raises Lazarus from the dead
Jn. 11:1-20

Reading to establish *the fourth level of imagery*, the integral level of my own experience. Here I find my own essence or "groundedness." I find a sense of new commitment to and communion with social, ecological and spiritual order. I gaze at the scene with love and become open to an awareness of order and presence.

[1.] Now a man was ill, Lazarus from Bethany, the village of Mary and her sister Martha. [2] Mary was the one who had anointed the Lord with perfumed oil and dried his feet with her hair; it was her brother Lazarus who was ill. [3] So the sisters sent word to him, saying, "Master, the one you love is ill." [4] When Jesus heard this he said, "This illness is not to end in death, but is for the glory of God, that the Son of God may be glorified through it."[5] Now Jesus loved Martha and her sister and Lazarus. [6] So that when he heard that he was ill, he remained for two days in the place where he was. [7] Then after this he said to his disciples "Let us go back to Judea." [8] The disciples said to him, "Rabbi, the Jews were just trying to stone you, and you want to go back there?" [9] Jesus answered, "Are there not twelve hours in a day? If one walks during the day, he does not stumble, because he sees the light of this world.[10] But if one walks at night, he stumbles, because the light is not in him." [11] He said this, and then told them," Our friend Lazarus is asleep, but I am going to awaken him." [12] So the disciples said to him, "Master, if he is asleep he will be saved." [13] But Jesus was talking about his death, while they thought that he meant ordinary sleep. [14] So then Jesus said to them clearly, "Lazarus has died. [15] And I am glad for you that I was not there, that you may believe. Let us go to him." [16] So Thomas called Didymus, said to his fellow disciples "Let us also go to die with him." [17] When Jesus arrived, he found that Lazarus had already been in the tomb for four days. [18] Now Bethany was near Jerusalem, only about two miles away. [19] And many of the Jews had come to Martha and Mary to comfort them about their brother. [20] When Martha heard that Jesus was coming, she went to meet him, but Mary sat at home.

Seven Signs

RESPONSE AT THE INTEGRAL LEVEL OF IMAGERY

Herein I descend to a level of awareness in which I experience my own true essence or the 'Ground of my Being'. Here I'm enabled to find The Holy Grail', the Cornucopia, and to courageously "launch out into the deep". I experience that the universe outside, is reflected on the inside, and I find that Great Nature is contained within both. Images and archetypes can become for me structural forms that mirror to me, the wider reality of the energy of life. Persons portrayed in this human event experienced a new sightedness.

> In the light of the life, death and resurrection of Jesus, what does this text say to me?

I become aware of possibilities of involvement in deep contemplation, in works of compassion, of hospitality and generosity in response to the Risen Presence and power of that which the renowned Tielhard de Chardin called "The Within".

I pray for the grace to wholeheartedly respond to that Echo within. Those things that I have sensed, recalled and identified with, connect with a still point and are accessed through this SIGN.

> What do I say to JESUS who speaks to me in this text?

Seven Signs

Reflection to listen.

I listen to 'felt' responses to the issues that this story encourages in me to effect **action.**

What is it that I yearn to move toward?

What does the Spirit of Jesus want me to do today?

Why did the 'Holy Spirit choose this **event** to effect an ACTION of Jesus?

I LISTEN to my heart, the core of my being, where the Holy Spirit moves and I speak to Jesus about any things that connect me with this Sign of Jesus.

I record the words, images or feelings that connect me with the compassionate feelings and actions of Jesus.

Words	*Feelings*	*Images*
↓	↓	↓

Seven Signs

Reflection for insight.

I have some insights regarding my own values and attitudes that compare with the attitudes of compassion, hospitality and inclusion of Jesus toward persons present in this event.

I have become aware that He has the desire and power to help me to improve or to develop my personal relationships with my family, my friends and with Him from the following:

A WORD from scripture	A value that Jesus exhibits
Some unique relationship that Jesus communicates.	Some personal enlightenment

Seven Signs

I reflect on the **values** that the characters portray for **insight** to clarify my own values.

Which characters?	What values do they exhibit?
_____	_____
_____	_____
_____	_____
_____	_____
_____	_____

I choose to 'step' into the persona or character of_____
with whom I empathise to become conscious that . . .

I too am called to:

- a new awareness
  e.g. _____
  _____

- a new
  perception _____
  _____

- a new enlightenment
  concerning _____
  _____

- a new application ie, action
  _____
  _____

Seven Signs

Some suggestions to **journal** my response to this Sign of Jesus.

Identification with the persona—

- I "become" one of the characters in this event and write "in role" from their perspective or perspectives.

I write—(of what happened in heart today when I met Jesus in this event).

- a letter to God, to Mary, or to my own inner spirit.
- a poem, prayer or lyric.
- about my reactions to any specific character.

I identify—

- the people I celebrate who are in my life.
- what I celebrate in my own life.
- my own differences.
- my own uniqueness.
- my own gifts, talents and capabilities.

I construct—

- what the symbols in this scene resemble or mean for me. (e.g. empty jars, wine, bread)
- a crossword puzzle with both questions and answers.

I draw—

- symbols that I've identified as having meaning that connect me with this Sign.

Seven Signs

Journal in response to the raising of Lazarus. (part 1)   Date: / / .

_____

_____

_____

_____

_____

_____

_____

_____

_____

_____

_____

_____

_____

_____

_____

_____

_____

Seven Signs

Resolution

I ask for the grace to respond enthusiastically to the revelation **I** have received in this reflection on God's love, His intimacy and His power. I ask that God's name will be honoured and that God's reign will be achieved in me and in all people everywhere, as I make my resolutions.

	Long term goal	Short term goal	Daily goal
What is the goal?			
Why?			
Time frame of realising this goal			
I visualise myself achieving my goals and draw this.			

I make a personal affirmation _____

I isolate a mantra from the reading _____

Seven Signs

Lazarus-called and raised to life.
Mandala

I may have become aware of a central and powerful meaning from focusing on this event.

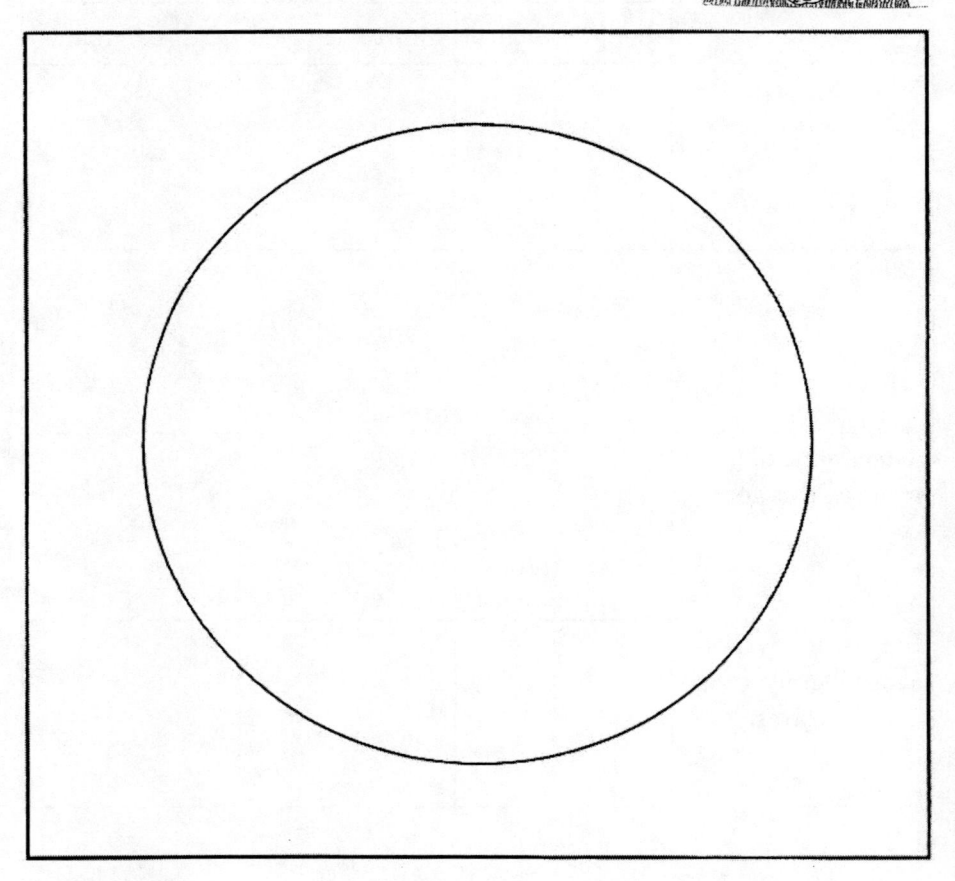

Perhaps to draw a meaningful symbol (that typifies, represents or recalls some idea or quality), within the mandala may register for me the power I've derived from considering or contemplating this sign.

Seven Signs

Recapitulation or Examine.

From reading about and contemplating the actions and attitudes of Jesus in this significant event, I have realised an aspect of the true nature and identity of Jesus-viz _____

This realisation has the power to call me to respond using the four functions of my psyche, to sense, to think, to feel emotionally and to use my intuition. It is this last function of intuition that *connects* me with the *risen presence of Jesus,* transferred to me in this event and that invites me to grow in love, patience, kindness and service toward my family and also within my social and professional world.

I visualise myself engaged in a particular situation where I am empowered to pray, to act with hospitality, compassion or patience in response to the persons whom I encounter in my life today. I draw this mental projection of myself acting positively, within the circular diagram.

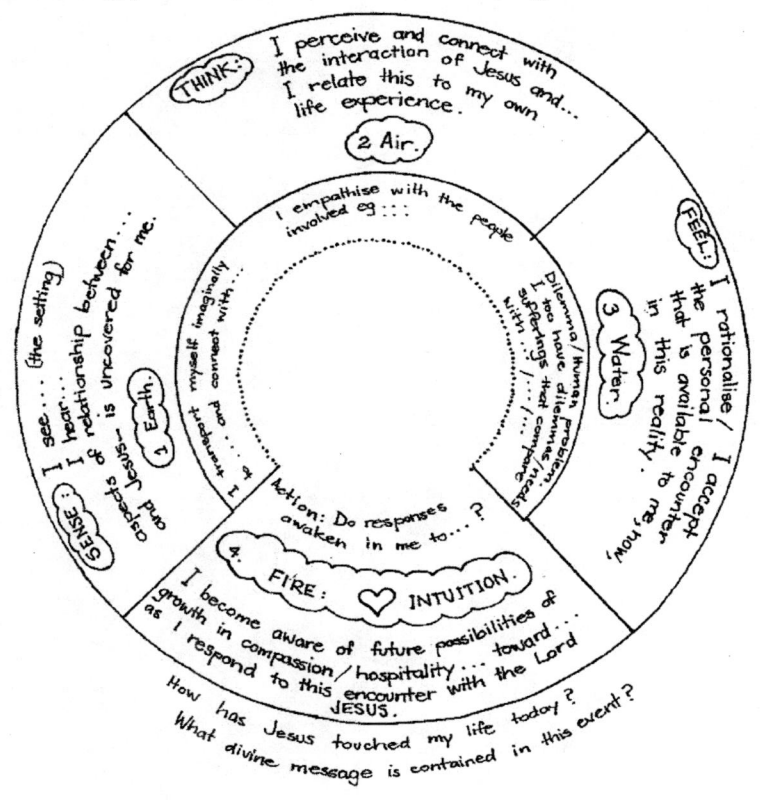

NOTES

NOTES

SEVEN SIGNS

JESUS RAISES LAZARUS FROM THE DEAD

PART SEVEN (b)—SEVENTH SIGN

Read—Jesus called forth Lazarus from death. Jn 11:28-44
Read—Outline the narrative
Read—Highlight any significant words or phrases
Read—Observe personal responses/relationships of characters

Reflect—Listen to your felt responses.
Reflect—Insights/values clarified.

Journal—Write "in role as any chosen character"
Resolution—Affirmation/prayer or mantra
Mandala—Draw essential idea.
Notes—Any connected personal ideas

Seventh Sign

Jesus raises Lazarus from the dead.
Jn. 11:28-44

Reading to establish the literal meaning using the first level of imagery, the surface or sensory level.

²⁸ When she had said this, she went and called her sister Mary secretly, saying, "The teacher is here and is asking for you." ²⁹ As soon as she heard this, she rose quickly and went to him. ³⁰ For Jesus had not yet come into the village, but was still where Martha had met him. ³¹ So when the Jews who were with her in the house comforting her saw Mary get up quickly and go out, they followed her, presuming that she was going to the tomb to weep there. ³² When Mary came to where Jesus was and saw him, she fell at his feet and said to him, "Lord, if you had been here, my brother would not have died." ³³ When Jesus saw her weeping and the Jews who had come with her weeping, he became perturbed and deeply troubled, ³⁴ and said, "Where have you laid him?" They said to him "Sir, come and see." ³⁵ and Jesus wept. ³⁶ So the Jews said, "See how he loved him." ³⁷ But some of them said, "Could not the one who opened the eyes of the blind man have done something so that this man would not have died?" ³⁸ So Jesus, perturbed again, came to the tomb. It was a cave, and a stone lay across it. ³⁹ Jesus said, "Take away the stone." Martha, the dead man's sister, said to him, "Lord, by now there will be a stench; he has been dead for four days." ⁴⁰ Jesus said to her, "Did I not tell you that if you believe you will see the glory of God?" ⁴¹ So they took away the stone. And Jesus raised his eyes and said," Father, I thank you for hearing me. ⁴² I know that you always hear me; but because of the crowd here, I have said this, that they may believe that you sent me."⁴³ And when he had said this, he cried out in a loud voice, "Lazarus, come out!" ⁴⁴ The dead man came out, tied hand and foot with burial bands, and his face was wrapped in a cloth. So Jesus said to them, "Untie him and let him go."

RESPONSE AT THE SENSORY LEVEL OF IMAGERY

Setting:.

- Where did the event take place?
- When (historically)?
- What was the event?

Characters;

- Who are the major characters?
- Who are the minor characters?

Dilemma or human problem;

- What was the problem?
- Who was affected by the problem?

Action.

- Who initiated a response?
- How did Jesus respond to this human problem?

Conclusion:

- What were the final results for the major characters?
- What were the results for minor characters?

What do I sense from this scene?

Seventh Sign

Jesus raises Lazarus from the dead.
Jn. 11:28-44

Reading to establish the *second level of imagery,* the recollective/analytic level to evoke personal connected memories

[28] When she had said this, she went and called her sister Mary secretly, saying, "The teacher is here and is asking for you." [29] As soon as she heard this, she rose quickly and went to him. [30] For Jesus had not yet come into the village, but was still where Martha had met him. [31] So when the Jews who were with her in the house comforting her saw Mary get up quickly and go out, they followed her, presuming that she was going to the tomb to weep there. [32] When Mary came to where Jesus was and saw him, she fell at his feet and said to him, "Lord, if you had been here, my brother would not have died." [33] When Jesus saw her weeping and the Jews who had come with her weeping, he became perturbed and deeply troubled, [34] and said, "Where have you laid him?" They said to him "Sir, come and see." [35] and Jesus wept. [36] So the Jews said, "See how he loved him." [37] But some of them said, "Could not the one who opened the eyes of the blind man have done something so that this man would not have died?" [38] So Jesus, perturbed again, came to the tomb. It was a cave, and a stone lay across it. [39] Jesus said, "Take away the stone." Martha, the dead man's sister, said to him, "Lord, by now there will be a stench; he has been dead for four days." [40] Jesus said to her, "Did I not tell you that if you believe you will see the glory of God?" [41] So they took away the stone. And Jesus raised his eyes and said," Father, I thank you for hearing me. [42] I know that you always hear me; but because of the crowd here, I have said this, that they may believe that you sent me."[43] And when he had said this, he cried out in a loud voice, "Lazarus, come out!" [44] The dead man came out, tied hand and foot with burial bands, and his face was wrapped in a cloth. So Jesus said to them, "Untie him and let him go."

RESPONSE AT THE RECOLLECTIVE—ANALYTIC LEVEL OF IMAGERY.

Here I study my own past, my problems and my potentialities. Memories both verbal and visual are accessed as I analyse this narrative. I resonate parallels in my own life.

Narrative Structure: Diagram

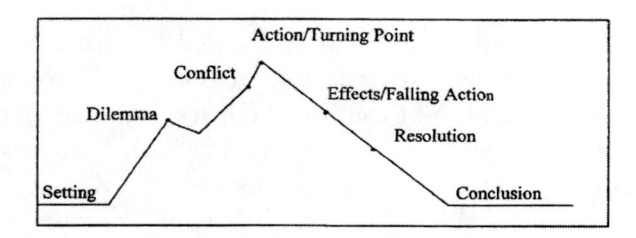

```
                    Action/Turning Point
         Conflict
                       Effects/Falling Action
    Dilemma
                          Resolution
Setting
                             Conclusion
```

Setting:
- I transport myself imaginally to the place. _____
- I connect with a character of my choice viz _____

Characters—
- I empathise with a certain person viz _____
  or persons viz _____
  _____

The dilemma/human problem;
- I accept this as my own problem.
- I experience the suffering.
- I take on board the needs.

Action—
- I recognize my own potential to solve problems, to be proactive and to decide in favour of goal setting and positive intention to act.

Conclusion
- What are the final results for me from my identification with my chosen character?

What have I become more aware of?
- What message have I found in this scene that connects with memories in my own life experience?

Seventh Sign

Jesus raises Lazarus from the dead.
Jn. 11:28-44

Reading to establish the *third level of imagery*, the symbolic level. This enables me to connect with mythical and archetypal figures. Here I find that symbols can have relevance to my life.

[28] When she had said this, she went and called her sister Mary secretly, saying, "The teacher is here and is asking for you." [29] As soon as she heard this, she rose quickly and went to him. [30] For Jesus had not yet come into the village, but was still where Martha had met him. [31] So when the Jews who were with her in the house comforting her saw Mary get up quickly and go out, they followed her, presuming that she was going to the tomb to weep there. [32] When Mary came to where Jesus was and saw him, she fell at his feet and said to him, "Lord, if you had been here, my brother would not have died." [33] When Jesus saw her weeping and the Jews who had come with her weeping, he became perturbed and deeply troubled, [34] and said, "Where have you laid him?" They said to him "Sir, come and see." [35] and Jesus wept. [36] So the Jews said, "See how he loved him." [37] But some of them said, "Could not the one who opened the eyes of the blind man have done something so that this man would not have died?" [38] So Jesus, perturbed again, came to the tomb. It was a cave, and a stone lay across it. [39] Jesus said, "Take away the stone." Martha, the dead man's sister, said to him, "Lord, by now there will be a stench; he has been dead for four days." [40] Jesus said to her, "Did I not tell you that if you believe you will see the glory of God?" [41] So they took away the stone. And Jesus raised his eyes and said," Father, I thank you for hearing me. [42] I know that you always hear me; but because of the crowd here, I have said this, that they may believe that you sent me."[43] And when he had said this, he cried out in a loud voice, "Lazarus, come out!" [44] The dead man came out, tied hand and foot with burial bands, and his face was wrapped in a cloth. So Jesus said to them, "Untie him and let him go."

Seven Signs

RESPONSE AT THE SYMBOLIC LEVEL OF IMAGERY

I highlight words or phrases that symbolize and reflect patterns in my own personal life and its context. These symbolic images move me beyond my own personal-particular, toward more universal formulations. Here I'm able to experience a sense of continuity with evolutionary and historic process. I may identify with archetypical figures that have relevance to my own life and to my own problems.

Rational evaluation:

- I "become" this archetypal character to experience the facts of the situation, the values and relationship between this person and Jesus.
- I transfer this imaginal experience to my own real life situation.
- I observe the responsive action of Jesus toward _____
- I identify with the feelings of this character toward Jesus _____
- I observe the actions of other major characters _____
- I identify with the feelings of Jesus to this person _____
- I too participate in the feelings, needs and responses of the characters with whom I have chosen to identify.

The feelings and needs of the characters were connected, so that a final result occurred at that time and in that place.

From this consideration I choose a symbol that has power to recall for me the images that are now imprinted in my senses, in my memory and in my experience.

> I draw and label my chosen symbol.

The symbols I've selected have relevance to my own life as they represent my connection with my consciousness of sources of deep knowing and the reality of creative processes

Seventh Sign

Jesus raises Lazarus from the dead.
Jn. 11:28-44

Reading to establish *the fourth level of imagery,* the integral level of my own experience. Here I find my own essence or "groundedness." I find a sense of new commitment to and communion with social, ecological and spiritual order. I gaze at the scene with love and become open to an awareness of order and presence.

²⁸ When she had said this, she went and called her sister Mary secretly, saying, "The teacher is here and is asking for you." ²⁹ As soon as she heard this, she rose quickly and went to him. ³⁰ For Jesus had not yet come into the village, but was still where Martha had met him. ³¹ So when the Jews who were with her in the house comforting her saw Mary get up quickly and go out, they followed her, presuming that she was going to the tomb to weep there. ³² When Mary came to where Jesus was and saw him, she fell at his feet and said to him, "Lord, if you had been here, my brother would not have died." ³³ When Jesus saw her weeping and the Jews who had come with her weeping, he became perturbed and deeply troubled, ³⁴ and said, "Where have you laid him?" They said to him "Sir, come and see." ³⁵ and Jesus wept. ³⁶ So the Jews said, "See how he loved him." ³⁷ But some of them said, "Could not the one who opened the eyes of the blind man have done something so that this man would not have died?" ³⁸ So Jesus, perturbed again, came to the tomb. It was a cave, and a stone lay across it. ³⁹ Jesus said, "Take away the stone." Martha, the dead man's sister, said to him, "Lord, by now there will be a stench; he has been dead for four days." ⁴⁰ Jesus said to her, "Did I not tell you that if you believe you will see the glory of God?" ⁴¹ So they took away the stone. And Jesus raised his eyes and said," Father, I thank you for hearing me. ⁴² I know that you always hear me; but because of the crowd here, I have said this, that they may believe that you sent me."⁴³ And when he had said this, he cried out in a loud voice, "Lazarus, come out!" ⁴⁴ The dead man came out, tied hand and foot with burial bands, and his face was wrapped in a cloth. So Jesus said to them, "Untie him and let him go."

Seven Signs

RESPONSE AT THE INTEGRAL LEVEL OF IMAGERY

Herein I descend to a level of awareness in which I experience my own true essence or the 'Ground of my Being'. Here I'm enabled to find The Holy Grail', the Cornucopia, and to courageously "launch out into the deep". I experience that the universe outside, is reflected on the inside, and I find that Great Nature is contained within both. Images and archetypes can become for me structural forms that mirror to me, the wider reality of the energy of life. Persons portrayed in this human event experienced a new sightedness.

> In the light of the life, death and resurrection of Jesus, what does this text say to me?

I become aware of possibilities of involvement in deep contemplation, in works of compassion, of hospitality and generosity in response to the Risen Presence and power of that which the renowned Tielhard de Chardin called "The Within".

I pray for the grace to wholeheartedly respond to that Echo within. Those things that I have sensed, recalled and identified with, connect with a still point and are accessed through this SIGN.

> What do I say to JESUS who speaks to me in this text?

Seven Signs

Reflection to listen.

I listen to 'felt' responses to the issues that this story encourages in me to effect **action**.

What is it that I yearn to move toward?

What does the Spirit of Jesus want me to do today?

Why did the 'Holy Spirit choose this **event** to effect an ACTION of Jesus?

I LISTEN to my heart, the core of my being, where the Holy Spirit moves and I speak to Jesus about any things that connect me with this Sign of Jesus.

I record the words, images or feelings that connect me with the compassionate feelings and actions of Jesus.

Words	*Feelings*	*Images*
↓	↓	↓

Seven Signs

Reflection for insight.

I have some insights regarding my own values and attitudes that compare with the attitudes of compassion, hospitality and inclusion of Jesus toward persons present in this event.

I have become aware that He has the desire and power to help me to improve or to develop my personal relationships with my family, my friends and with Him from the following:

A WORD from scripture	A value that Jesus exhibits
Some unique relationship that Jesus communicates.	Some personal enlightenment

Seven Signs

I reflect on the **values** that the characters portray for **insight** to clarify my own values.

Which characters?	What values do they exhibit?
_____	_____
_____	_____
_____	_____
_____	_____

I choose to 'step' into the persona or character of_____
with whom I empathise to become conscious that . . .

I too am called to:

- a new awareness
  e.g. _____

- a new
  perception _____

- a new enlightenment
  concerning _____
  _____

- a new application ie, action
  _____

Seven Signs

Some suggestions to **journal** my response to this Sign of Jesus.

Identification with the persona—

- I "become" one of the characters in this event and write "in role" from their perspective or perspectives.

I write—(of what happened in heart today when I met Jesus in this event).

- a letter to God, to Mary, or to my own inner spirit.
- a poem, prayer or lyric.
- about my reactions to any specific character.

I identify—

- the people I celebrate who are in my life.
- what I celebrate in my own life.
- my own differences.
- my own uniqueness.
- my own gifts, talents and capabilities.

I construct—

- what the symbols in this scene resemble or mean for me. (e.g. empty jars, wine, bread)
- a crossword puzzle with both questions and answers.

I draw—

- symbols that I've identified as having meaning that connect me with this Sign.

Seven Signs

Journal in response to the raising of Lazarus. (part 2)   Date: / / .

Seven Signs

Resolution

I ask for the grace to respond enthusiastically to the revelation I have received in this reflection on God's love, His intimacy and His power. I ask that God's name will be honoured and that God's reign will be achieved in me and in all people everywhere, as I make my resolutions.

	Long term goal	Short term goal	Daily goal
What is the goal?			
Why?			
Time frame of realising this goal			
I visualise myself achieving my goals and draw this.			

I make a personal affirmation _____

I isolate a mantra from the reading _____

Seven Signs

Lazarus-called and raised to life.
Mandala

I may have become aware of a central and powerful meaning from focusing on this event.

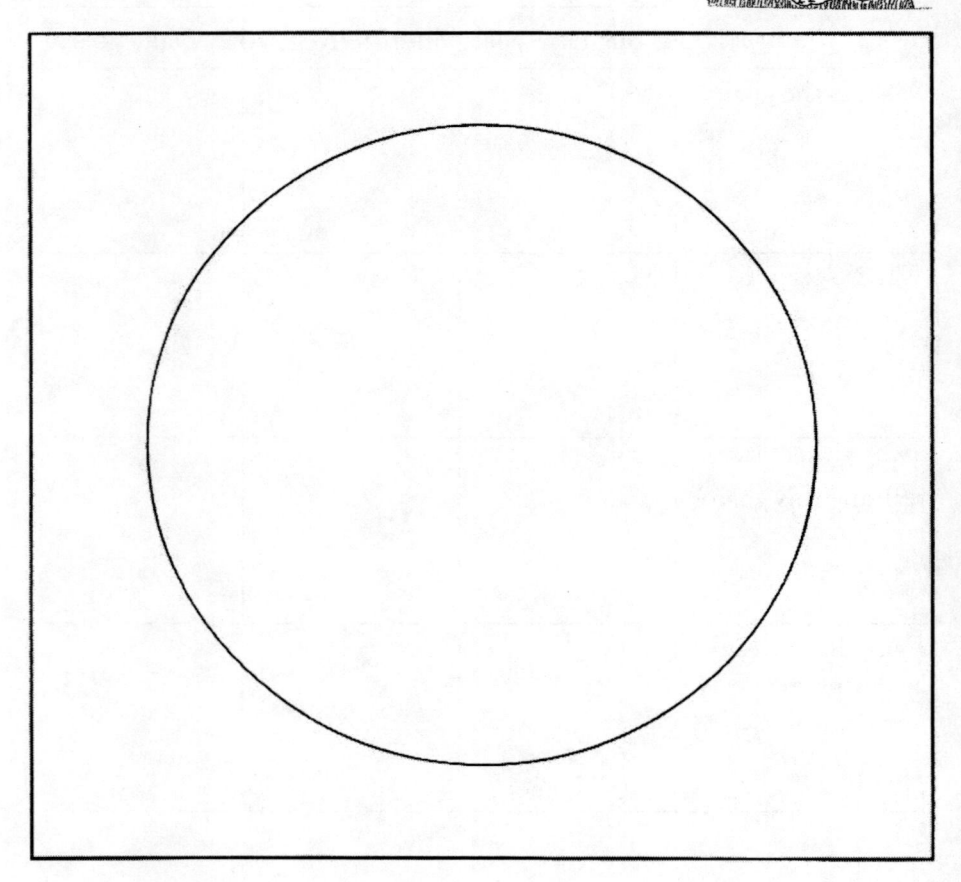

Perhaps to draw a meaningful symbol (that typifies, represents or recalls some idea or quality), within the mandala may register for me the power I've derived from considering or contemplating this sign.

Seven Signs

Recapitulation or Examine.

From reading about and contemplating the actions and attitudes of Jesus in this significant event, I have realised an aspect of the true nature and identity of Jesus-viz _____

This realisation has the power to call me to respond using the four functions of my psyche, to sense, to think, to feel emotionally and to use my intuition. It is this last function of intuition that *connects* me with the *risen presence of Jesus,* transferred to me in this event and that invites me to grow in love, patience, kindness and service toward my family and also within my social and professional world.

I visualise myself engaged in a particular situation where I am empowered to pray, to act with hospitality, compassion or patience in response to the persons whom I encounter in my life today. I draw this mental projection of myself acting positively, within the circular diagram.

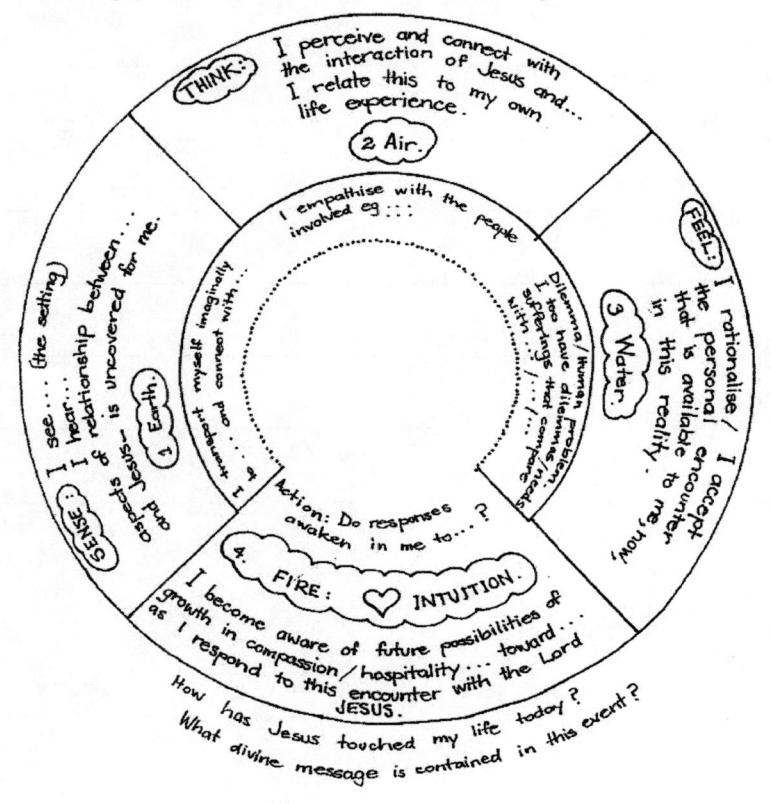

Circular diagram with four quadrants:

- **THINK — 2. Air:** I perceive and connect with the interaction of Jesus and... I relate this to my own life experience.
- **FEEL — 3. Water:** I rationalise / I accept the personal encounter that is available to me in this reality, now.
- **SENSE — 1. Earth:** I see... I hear... (the setting) relationship between... two aspects of Jesus... is uncovered for me.
- **FIRE — 4. INTUITION:** I become aware of future possibilities of growth in compassion/hospitality... as I respond to this encounter with the Lord JESUS.

Inner ring prompts: I empathise with the people involved eg...; I too have dilemma/human problem/ feelings that compare... suffering with...; I project myself imaginatively and connect with...; Action: Do responses awaken in me to...?

Outer prompts: How has Jesus touched my life today? What divine message is contained in this event?

NOTES

NOTES

LIST OF REFERENCES

Borysenko, Joan. *Guilt is the Teacher, Love is the Lesson.* New York: Crucible, 1990.

Brown, R. Fitzmyer, J, Murphy, R. (Editors) *The Jerome Biblical Commentary.* London: Cassel Ltd., 1980.

Catucci, Thomas. *Time with Jesus.* Indiana : Ave Maria Press, 1993.

Campbell, Joseph. *The Hero with a Thousand Faces.* London: Fontana Press, 1993.

Fallon, Michael. *The Gospel according to St John.* Kensington, NSW: Chevalier Press,

Frankl, Viktor. *Man's Search for Meaning.* New York: Pocket Books, 1985.

Houston, Jean. *The Search for The Beloved. Journeys In Sacred Psychology.* Los Angeles: Jeremy P. Tarcher, Inc., 1987

Houston, Jean. *The Possible Human.* New York: Jeremy P Tarcher/Putman, 1982.

Jung, Carl. (Editor), *Man and His Symbols.* London: Picador, 1978.

Myss, Caroline. *Anatomy of the Spirit. The Seven Stages of Power and Healing.* New York: Harmony Books, 1996

Ralph, Margaret. *Discovering the Gospels.* New Jersey: Paulist Press, 1990.

Robertson, Robin. *Introducing Jungian, Psychology._* Dublin: Gill & Macmillan Ltd., 1992.

Stanley, David. *I Encountered God. The Spiritual Exercises with the Gospel of St. John.* St. Louis: The Institute of Jesuit Sources, 1986

Teilhard de Chardin. Pierre. *Hymn of the Universe,* New York: Harper and Row, 1965

New American Bible. School and Church Edition, Fireside Bible Publishers

Wichita, Kansas. *www.FiresideBibles.com*